TO Fred & Sharon My Brother &
Sister — Reading this Book
will be a _____ _____
God Bless Thank You

# I'm Still Standing

# I'm Still Standing

## Raymond Hicks

CreateSpace Independent Publishing Platform
2015

# Chapter One

I sat shackled, looking on helplessly as my whole world fell apart before my eyes.

Stone-faced uniformed officers were searching every inch of my house as I watched. None of them made eye contact with me; they walked back and forth as if I were invisible. I shifted uncomfortably as the cold steel of the handcuffs seemed to dig into my skin. The air was so thick and heavy I feared my lungs would collapse beneath its crushing weight. I winced at the sour, metallic taste in my mouth. I'd accidentally bit my tongue when they'd slammed me to the floor of my own living room.

I'd noticed all the unmarked cars scattered through my neighborhood when I pulled up in front of my house that June afternoon in 2000, but I had no idea they were there for me. How could I? Now my own house, my private domain, had been violated. I closed my eyes. God, is this really happening? I could hear shuffling and banging noises coming from every room as they overturned furniture and opened every drawer. What were they looking for? The sound of shattered glass from the kitchen jarred my eyes open and I straightened up suddenly. A few of the deputies stopped cold in their tracks as they eyed me carefully. One of them, a scruffy-

1

looking, heavy-set man with steel-blue eyes, rested his hand on his gun holster. I stiffened my body to keep myself calm.

I wasn't going to give anyone with an itchy trigger finger a reason. My eyes roamed over the framed portraits hanging on the walls. The smiling faces of my wife and daughters wrenched my heart and I could feel anger coursing through me like hot venom. I forced myself to look away from the family pictures. Looking at them only made my rage escalate further.

I looked up at the sound of approaching footsteps. A tall, dark-skinned deputy with coal-black eyes and a buzzcut walked toward me. I recognized him immediately. It was Myers, a deputy I had done a few late-night shifts with some time ago. He opened his mouth and began to read me my Miranda rights.

My heart sank as the realization of what this meant hit me. "I'm innocent," I wanted to interrupt him. But I knew better. This had all been planned.

I was arrested by Broward Sheriff's Office deputies on the charge of trafficking 350 kilograms of cocaine to various states and then escorted by Deputy Brown to district five for booking (see Appendix, p. 1, Doc. #1). Later that afternoon I was transported to the city jail and placed in confinement. The next morning I was escorted by marshals to the magistrates' court where the judge gave the order to detain me, saying I was a threat to society. I was escorted back to the holding cell and minutes later the marshals transported me to the federal detention center. They took all my personal items; I was fingerprinted, strip-searched, and told to place all my clothing in a box to be shipped back to my residence. Shortly after, in prison garb, I was escorted to solitary confinement, and the officers put me in a place called the Shu (the "hole") in the federal prison, which is similar to a doghouse where you shower, eat, and defecate. I was locked up for several months until I began to act like a vicious lion in a cage looking for prey. This hole in the wall was very dark, admitting no sunlight, and was very cold. The officers fed me through an opening and they allowed me to use the phone only every seven days to call my attorney.

I remembered reading about a man named Ray Lewis, who was locked up for something he didn't do. He channeled his anger into doing pushups–he worked up to 1,500 pushups per day. I took the same approach to keep from hurting myself or the officers. I'd work out hard until I would eventually be able to fall asleep.

I witnessed guys throwing wet tissue, urine, and feces out of the hole. Anxiety and depression set in so heavily that I began to talk to myself and the wall would respond, which I know is referred to as hallucinating. There is an emergency button inside the cell that you push only if there's an emergency. I reached the point where I began pushing the button repeatedly because I wanted to fight with the officers, inmates, or any staff member I could lay hands on if given the opportunity. Their response was, "Inmate Hicks, chill out."

My reply was, "Come in here and make me."

This entire ordeal reminded me, first, of Sidney Lumet's movie "Serpico," starring Al Pacino, who went undercover to expose corruption in the force and then suffered isolation from his friends and co-workers. It also reminded me of Ruben "Hurricane" Carter when he was thrown into the hole, as well as "Training Day" with Denzel Washington, and also "American Gangster" because of my own belligerent behavior.

I was removed from the Shu, perhaps in retaliation, and placed in General Population, which can be a death threat to an officer. But I knew it meant that I could begin to have visits from my family, so I didn't object. While I was in solitary, I'd had no contact with my wife or children.

I was placed on the "crazy floor," 7 West; my state of mind affected my whole body–I had no control over my bowels, and found myself using the toilet five times a day. I went from 285 pounds to 230 pounds within two weeks. I was approached by an inmate, a guy who stood about 6 feet 4 inches and weighed 270 pounds and who had seen my picture paraded over newscasts. He said to me, "You're that f!@#ing cop!"

"You have a problem with me?"

"Yes, I hate cops."

Another inmate who recognized me from my work at the county jail heard us talking and said, "You

don't want to mess with Hicks"– except he said "f!@#
Hicks."

I went to my cell and put my bed together, returned
to the day room and informed the man, "If you have a
problem with me, you and I can go into the room, close
the door and handle the problem." We both agreed and
went into the cell and had a major altercation. Thirty
minutes later he went to the officer and asked to be moved
to another unit. After that incident I calmed down and
became more rational. I came closer to God, bringing
forth His word and conveying His message to other
brothers. On the other hand, after that incident I saved
the metal top of a sardine can from the commissary,
cleaned and sharpened it, and carried it in my pocket.

Unbelievably, sixteen and a half months passed.

While in the federal detention center in Miami,
I was surrounded by white toilets and graffiti-laced
walls. I sat on a board-hard bunk and stared at the bars
of sunlight on the floor near my feet. Picture this: it's
March 25, 2001, the time is 10 p.m. and I'm sitting in
my cell thinking to myself, "How could a person like
me be sitting here locked up? My toilet doesn't work,
has not worked for five days now, so my roommate and
I are forced to live here under appalling conditions.
Most of the guys here know that I used to be a deputy
sheriff–eight of the guys in my section I'd once arrested.
I'd put them in jail, and now they were my roommates!
So I'd find them laughing at me because of my present

situation, but despite my living conditions and the circumstances I'm facing, I'm still holding on to God's unchanging hand; He said that He will never leave me nor forsake me. There are times when I look up and say, 'Lord, Lord why me? I always wanted to do the best job I could do as an honest deputy,' and the reply I received was, 'Raymond, why not you?'"

So many people are terrified by incarceration. Family members are hanging up on them, wives divorcing them, no letters are coming in, and no money for commissary. Anxiety and depression take such a toll on so many brothers' lives here that most of them are taking heavy medications just to get by.

I can remember the first time one of the officers woke me up and told me that I had visitors. I walked to the laundry room and watched my family pull up and park on the side of the street. I watched them standing in a very long line; this would be repeated over time; there would be times when the weather was unforgiving and it rained on them since there were no outdoor awnings.

Usually, the officers would escort me and other expectant inmates to the visiting area where we would await the arrival of our families. Upon arrival, my wife and kids would begin to tell me how they were mistreated by the officers who checked for contraband and other miscellaneous items that were prohibited within the facility. For example, I recall my daughters Rayven and Martrice, telling me that as they walked through the metal detectors the alarm would sound because of the various hairpins they wore in their hair, and then they'd be asked to remove their shoes and other pieces of clothing. My wife, Patrice, would start in on the financial constraints that she and my daughters faced; as a matter of fact they would have only enough change to purchase one or two things from the vending machines during visits. I became infuriated but knew that I had to remain calm so that my family wouldn't see me lose my composure.

Thinking back, I remember that my children would always ask me, "Daddy, when are you coming home?" and I would say, "Soon." Weeks, months, and eventually a year and a half went by and my response was still the same. "Soon."

What kept me sane was the lifeline I felt to my wife. I remember the words Patrice said to me while I was held at the federal detention center in Miami: "I'm here for you." And that was true. I know how she and my kids suffered when I was removed from our home and the difficult situations they faced. Some people were often not sure what to say to me, but Patrice was very practical and specific when she offered help. I remember her telling me that she had applied for $25,000 through her Thrift Saving Plan to pay attorneys' fees.

There were times when I would telephone just to say "I love you, and I've been thinking about you." I missed smelling her perfume, and the thought that it would be a long time before we were together again made me crumble inside. She is a great mom and primarily responsible for raising our kids, and she deserves all the credit for this job, which goes on 24/7.

I love looking into her big beautiful brown eyes and saying, "Patrice, I love you." It gives me a very special feeling to know that I'm sharing my life with someone who is not just my wonderful wife but also the greatest friend a person could ever have. She is a very hard worker, and I can only imagine how difficult it was to try to support the family on one income while I was away. She told me that she was forced to dig for quarters, nickels, dimes and pennies to use for groceries at Winn Dixie. She remembers that when she and my daughters were standing in line and counting out coins, the other patrons began laughing out loud.

At the center, I witnessed guys taking sleeping pills as if they were candy, sometimes sleeping for several days without waking up. Most guys come in healthy, strong, and confident but after two or three months they're taking antidepressant medications. They begin talking to themselves, pacing up and down the rec yard, crying uncontrollably, and you want to help them. I thank God I never treated inmates badly because some of the inmates I'd once had authority over at the Broward County jail, I met again while I was incarcerated. We would eat at the same table.

I feel I put my time to good use once I settled in. I

spoke about faith, I helped guys prepare for their GEDs, and I sometimes acted as a jailhouse lawyer–an inmate who has never practiced law and has no formal training, but will informally assist other inmates in filing petitions and so forth. The U.S. Supreme Court has recognized the role jailhouse lawyers play. One of my "cases" comes to mind. A young man was visibly distressed by his situation, in which he was caught with point 7 grams (.7) of cocaine in his pockets. Now his lawyer was advising him to take a plea agreement because he was facing 13 years in prison.

Many blacks, unable to afford a high-powered lawyer, simply strike a plea bargain to avoid facing increasingly harsh sentences, and their lawyers take the easy way out, to the point where an accused person thinks this is the norm.

"You can't go to jail for 13 years for that!" I told him. The relief and excitement he felt lit up his face.

I prepared an argument for him, and he received a reduced sentence of three years, followed by a drug rehabilitation program which further cut his sentence in half. Later he told me his attorney asked him, "Who prepared this?"

"I just said another inmate, but I didn't use your name, because I didn't know whether it was O.K."

"You did the right thing, man. You're going to get through this," I assured him.

Although I'd been a law enforcement officer,

which could have been a death sentence in prison, most of the inmates recognized me and respected me at the center in Miami. They spoke highly of me, which made me feel good on the inside. My mother always told me, "Be careful how you treat people on your way up, because these might be the same people you meet on your way down." I thought that her statement was very true and not to be taken lightly.

I tried to be a model inmate, even helping to save the life of a prisoner who had a seizure. When an older man seemed to be failing after a fall, I alerted an officer. "He's getting worse," I reported again after nothing was done. I thought this was really serious, and I began to talk to the old man. "Have you accepted God as your Lord and Saviour?" I asked him. He managed to nod his head. When he died about ten minutes later, I felt I had helped him through the last rites, and I hoped that was a comfort. I sat by his side until I was told to leave.

They came and propped him in a wheelchair as if he was still alive and took him away, saying later that he died at the hospital. I just stared at the officer I had begged to help the old man. "No inmate ever died in jail!" he told me.

I ran into that same officer in a few years later when I was working for Homeland Security. "You look exactly like a man I used to know," he said.

"I am that man," I told him. "I'm Raymond Hicks."

"No!" he said, looking as if he'd seen a ghost.

There are so many people who are dying in jail and prison, but their family members will never know the cause of death because they never question, they never demand an investigation. They just accept what's told to them.

The federal system is totally different from that of the state. They have a practice that people in society are unfamiliar with. It's called "jumping on the bus." I know you as a reader are saying, "What does that mean?" Let me elaborate. It's when the district attorney and various agents come together with other inmates to say they know you, whether they know you or not. It's when they use other inmates to testify against you at trial or to the grand jury. These people become confidential informants and are protected by the government. Some of them receive reduced sentences, money and even a new identity. I'm informed that if you have a court-appointed attorney on the federal level and you take a plea, the district attorney will give your attorney a bonus. When I was a corrections officer no one could ever have told me that these types of activities went on–I wouldn't have believed them–but seeing it with my own eyes brought me to face reality.

I remember an older gentleman, Mr. James Watts, telling me at the Broward County jail when I was a deputy in 6 Delta, "Man, you don't know how it feels to be locked up." I responded by saying, "I know how you feel, Mr. Watts," even though of course I didn't. Once I was a federal prisoner locked up on fabricated charges, I realize what Mr. Watts was saying. To be quite honest, it took my own incarceration to understand what he was he was trying to convey to me.

# Chapter Two

The following is a list of events that have disillusioned me and darkened my life, me, a former corrections deputy, by taking away from me my liberty, and condemning me to be an inmate in the cells of the Federal Detention Center of Miami. I was arrested in Ft. Lauderdale on June 15, 2000, by several Broward sheriff's deputies who had been planning fabricated charges against me for a very long time. In a condensed format, here are some of the confrontations that preceded that event.

A) In 1990, internal affairs received a formal complaint in a letter from a female deputy stating that I had punched her in the back. Deputy Horace, an eyewitness, testified that no such an assault ever took place; he was present at the time of the alleged incident. The female deputy had made a rude comment about my mother. I told the woman in front of Horace, "The longest day you live, don't you ever disrespect my mother again." I received a written reprimand because of this complaint.

B) In 1992, I was ordered to confiscate a weapon from an inmate by Lt. Elkins and Lt. Crane. I was issued a bullet-proof jacket from master control and several ranking officers were issued shotguns; this was the only time that guns were permitted inside the jail. The special response team was deployed to the location to stand by at the jail stairwell. After I completed a cell shakedown, I reported that nothing was found. Afterward, I was informed by the administration that I would receive a favorable note in my personal file for this operation, but that never took place. The gun was later found in the laundry room. It had been passed from the inmate on the eighth floor to inmates who were picking up the dirty laundry.

C) In 1992-93 I was assigned to attend drill sergeant school in Ft. McCullum, Alabama. Two weeks into the program I reported to Sgt. Kim Columbus that my boots were causing blisters on my feet; I needed replacements of a larger boot size. Sgt. Columbus did not allow me to replace my boots and ordered me to continue with the program. Soon I could barely walk, and took the initiative to see Sgt. McGee to explain the situation. Sgt. McGee was shocked to see the condition of my feet and toes and summoned Sgt. Columbus. After confronting her with the issue, McGee told her that a private's medical concerns always demand urgent attention. Later Sgt. Columbus let me know that upon returning to B.S.O., she would deal with me on a personal level. Deputies Dallas Crew and Bruce Carson heard her make that threat. Following this, I received several written reprimands from Sgt. Columbus.

D) "Sexual harassment": Drill instructor Alexander

told a female cadet to tell me she loved me. My reply to the cadet was that such remark was unprofessional and disrespectful, but she continued repeating, "Hicks, I love you." I ordered her to perform some pushups for her comments. For that action, I received another written reprimand.

E) There was a "Failure to meet financial responsibility" written report: My mother had an outstanding balance of $285 to Mitsubishi. I made the payment and still received a written reprimand.

F) "Failure to properly feed a boot-camper": A written counsel report was placed in my file for the excessive feeding of a cadet. Cadet Heather Chapman wrote a letter stating she was never properly fed until she got sick. She was regularly given an extra meal tray by me in order to establish her normal weight (she had lost weight during her long-term addition to heroin). Sgt. Columbus tried her very best to get me fired from B.S.O. after this incident.

G) In B.S.O.'s first attempt to silence me, I was fired from the Broward Sheriff's Office in 1997, because of a complaint filed by an ex-convict who stated that I had threatened to arrest him (untrue). A Ft. Lauderdale police report was filed by my cousin against this individual after he physically assaulted her at a convenience store near her residence. I simply told him to stay away from my relative. I vigorously defended myself and my record, and was later reinstated in the job.

Over the years, I was a witness to several corrupt activities taking place within the Broward Sheriff's Office. I witnessed officers taking money from suspects, planting drugs, falsifying documents, gambling while on duty and more. I wasn't silent about these problems. Here are some of these incidents.

H) Theft of commissary money by superiors via subordinate staff: An estimated amount of about $500,000 had been stolen from commissary revenues. I was informed by a commissary supervisor that another supervisor was terminated for alleged corruption and dishonesty. He also stated that his name appeared on B. S. O. checks, which were being sent out to different family members. When I asked him who had direct access to his section, his answer was, "You must be crazy I'm an Italian, and Italians don't snitch."

I) Recently, a civilian who was assigned to the commissary department pocketed six hundred dollars to take care of personal matters. For this, his punishment was a three-day suspension; he was allowed to return to the department and was promoted several months later to confinement status, that is, overseeing people who are confined. On the other hand, Anita Byrd, a black female, was terminated on the spot for the alleged theft of thirty dollars out of property held for an inmate. Here are two clear examples of similar offenses, one committed by a white male, who gets a three-day suspension for taking six hundred dollars, and one by a black female, who loses her job for allegedly taking thirty dollars.

J) Here is another incident that clearly demonstrates favoritism and discrimination: Deputy Ray Williams, a black male, was fired several years ago for the use of narcotics. However, Deputy Gary Leonard, a white male, was taken to Sunshine Medical Center for treatment by Deputy Ken Prince after an anonymous caller stated he was using narcotics while working as a drill instructor at boot camp.

A positive indication of cocaine was found in Leonard's system after a blood test was conducted. He was asked by Internal Affairs to resign, but that was the end of it. To this date in time, Gary Leonard is still working as a law-enforcement officer in the Carolinas.

K) Just a few years back, director of detention Mr. Ferguson and his assistant (both black males) were terminated after a high-profile inmate escaped from a maximum security floor. However, Director Susan Campbell (a white female) was not terminated after an escape attempt caused the death of another high-profile inmate.

L) In 1997, I brought to the attention of the administration and Internal Affairs that it was wrong for the sheriff to authorize a conference on the first floor of the Public Safety Building, regularly held by Sgt. Roger and his wife and some 50 to 100 more deputies who were involved in what was basically a pyramid scheme.

Each member would put up $1,000 to hold a spot and have a chance at the jackpot. According to the Florida State statute book, this is a first-degree misdemeanor, but no one was brought up on any charges because too many people in higher positions were involved, so it was swept under the rug.

This list of events and many other issues and concerns are just a few of the personal harassments and improper punishments applied to me by B.S.O. administration and management staff members such as Sgt. Columbus, among others. Based on commendation letters and awards that I received during my dedicated years of service as a Broward Sheriff's deputy, my highly respected reputation and my civilian records of excellent services to the community, it is clear that something is wrong with the whole picture. It's my hope that a thorough investigation of the facts will commence at once, one that will bring out clear evidence of the fraudulent charges illegally brought against me.

I am a young black man who takes great pride in himself, and I did everything I could for those who were less fortunate–and without breaking the law.

Everything I did was batted down by a corrupt system that's notorious for misusing its authority. It's not what you know, but who you know–that's the American Way. Excuse my cynicism, but I think I've earned it.

There are a lot of officers who never develop interpersonal skills. They don't have enough opportunities to develop them, and then they don't get the training. I personally think it would benefit every man or woman who becomes a correctional officer or deputy sheriff to be mandated to spend one or two weeks incarcerated. Why? Because they will have the opportunity to experience what they put the inmates through. That experience will give them a different perspective on how they perceive people who are in their hands.

# Chapter Three

The nature and circumstances of the offenses against me escalated through time. I feel that an illegal search of my car without a search warrant or probable cause along with the subsequent 911 call I made to communications, the complaint form I submitted to Internal Affairs, and also my awareness of the corruption within the departments are what landed me at the federal detention center. The weight of the evidence against me rested primarily in the lies by a confidential informant, which I documented in an article titled "To Whom It May Concern."

The Broward Sheriff's Office employed me for fifteen years as a deputy sheriff, Since that time I have been discriminated against and have experienced retaliation from my peers. After filing several complaints about the illegal activities occurring in the workplace such as gambling and the operation of pyramids, I found myself transferred to another location.

On January 22, 1997, they found their excuse, and I was fired for misuse of authority. That charge resulted from contact I had with a male perpetrator who had an ongoing dispute with my female cousin in the community. I was not acting as deputy but as a concerned relative. I made contact with the individual and asked him not to take the law into his own hands, but instead to contact authorities if he had any further problems with my cousin. This individual then filed a false and fabricated report to Internal Affairs.

In the months after my firing, I applied for other police jobs in various municipalities; however, no one would hire me. I pursued a temporary position as a car salesman for Al Hendrickson Toyota. Meanwhile, I continued to contest my discrimination case with B.S.O.

On September 15, 1998, I was awarded my job back. However, there was no retroactive compensation for my dismissal, and my lawsuit was still pending. Upon my return, the retaliation continued as I experienced hostility both on and off the job.

In one instance of ongoing harassment, on December 15, 1999, my brother Bobby Hicks took my 1993 400 SEL Mercedes Benz to have it washed. A detective and a sergeant turned up and told my brother that they needed to search my vehicle. My brother responded, "Why?" but he went unanswered.

They instructed him to unlock the door and began to search my vehicle. In the process of searching, at least five witnesses looked on as they questioned my brother, asking him, "Where is the camera located?" "How can your brother afford this vehicle?" and muttering to each other, "The guy must be selling drugs." They concluded the search without finding anything.

Upon returning home my brother described to me

what had happened and I returned to the scene and called 911 to report the incident. I also informed the lieutenant from B.S.O. of the situation. After that, I filed a report with a sergeant from Internal Affairs that included names of the five witnesses. The sergeant from I.A., referring to the two officers who conducted the search, stated that there were numerous complaints against the pair. It should be noted that there was never an investigation or follow-up regarding this incident. The sergeant and his colleagues who searched my car later claimed that they had nothing to do with the investigation, even though at some point they reported "overhearing" a conversation in which I had asked deputies to run some names and obtain confidential police information to which I was not entitled.

Never happened.

During my civil trial, the sergeant admitted that he did not know that last bit to be factual, but that he did know there was supposedly a tape recording of me giving confidential information. When the tape was played for the judge and jury; they found out that it was not my voice on the tape but that of another deputy (see Appendix, pp. 2-4, Doc. #2).

Several weeks later an F.B.I. agent approached me regarding an arrangement to speak with him. Afterward, I called and left several messages for him. He finally called back and said, "My wife just gave birth," stating again that he still wanted to arrange a time to meet and

I said O.K. Several days later, while the F.B.I. agent was still temporizing, the Drug Task Force and other local police agents surrounded my residence and placed me under arrest. I was incarcerated for more than 16 months and was denied bail two times.

The allegations were all falsified and a tactic to silence my quest for justice. I was charged with conspiracy to traffic 350 kilograms of cocaine, the biggest shock of my life. The only drugs I ever sold were the small amounts provided by the B.S.O. for street work when I was assigned to the Drug Task Force.

My picture was paraded on every local newscast and newspaper. The false information has caused damage to my name and the career that I have worked so hard to attain. According to the State Attorney's office, there are taped conversations which were used to incriminate me. Yet the discovery phase of my case concluded that there was no evidence whatsoever linking me to the selling of drugs. It was also alleged that I was on more than 100 videotapes involving the trafficking of drugs: however, once again, I can't be found on these tapes. Amazing how much evidence they claimed to have that for one reason or another could not be produced in court.

As I sat there at the Federal Detention Center I began to write. The first person I wrote to was the reporter from The Sun-Sentinel who printed the first article about me and my involvement, but to no avail. She would not listen to me. The American University of

Washington College of Law, Creflo Dollars Ministries, Jesse Duplantis Ministries, American Civil Liberties Union of Florida, NAACP, Jesus People Ministries, U.S. House of Representatives, Breakthrough Ministries, Innocence Project of the National Capital Region, National Association of Criminal Defense Lawyers, Ebony Magazine, Al Sharpton, U.S. Department of Justice, all received letters from me.

# Chapter Four

June 15, 2000, keeps echoing in the back of my head as I remember coming home from a busy day's work around 3:30 p.m. and resting a couple of hours before I went outside to work out and I noticed several unmarked cars at the Citgo gas station near my house. When the men hanging around saw me they all jumped into their cars and came speeding down 44th Street, so I said to myself, "What's going on?" and ran to the front of my home, and that's when several Broward Sheriff's deputies approached me and asked me my name. I told them Raymond Hicks. They said to me, "You're under arrest, put your hands behind your back," I complied with their instruction.

After I was restrained I asked them, "What is this about?" They said to me, "We'll tell you later," and Deputy Robshaw asked me "Where're your uniforms and ID's?" I replied, "They're in the house," and he told me I was being placed on suspension without pay until the case was over. My kids were screaming, "What are you doing to my father?" My wife was crying and patting her chest, trying to calm herself. My most pressing question was why me? Why is this happening to me?

I've done all I could to help my fellow co-workers,

helped people earn their GEDs, given time to less fortunate kids, senior citizens, and my family. I have held many assignments, and always did my best in any job. But now in an instant 15 years of hard work and dedication as well as my reputation had been ruined by a corrupt system.

This is what I have to say about the system. I'm totally frustrated with a law-enforcement system that puts young black people in jail for little or no reason at all. Officers are expected to maintain order, prevent crimes and serve the community. However, one problem is that the broad discretion exercised by officers can produce discrimination when these officers do not treat members of different racial and ethnic groups in the same way.

Blacks report being unnecessarily stopped, questioned or taunted by the police at least once in their lifetimes. I'm very concerned that I might teach my daughters to fear the very people I worked for, the people my tax dollars pay to protect them. I refuse to teach my daughters to exist amid fear and anxiety. I will make sure that they know if stopped by the police they should be respectful, courteous, and cooperative. And hopefully they'll be treated courteously. Not every officer deserves a bad rap.

As I came closer to God He came closer to me and said, "I'm not concerned about your present situation, Raymond; I have lost sheep out there and I need a Good

Shepherd to go and bring them to me." I know you as a reader are saying, What is this man talking about?" Let me explain further. It was predestined before I came out of my mother's womb that God would choose me to be that bright light shining at the federal detention center where they have a conviction rate of 98 percent. I informed my fellow inmates, "Don't be concerned about your case, concentrate on God and He will see you through." They all thought I was crazy, but little did they know I had a connection with my Heavenly Father whose name is Jesus Christ. I began to pray, to fast, to believe, and finally to have faith that God would deliver me from the life of imprisonment I was facing.

After more than 11 months of incarceration, my attorney called me downstairs for a visit and informed me that the prosecutor wanted to offer me 16 1/2 months, meaning I would have to testify against the five codefendants who were named along with me in the indictment. I informed my attorney that I wouldn't have taken time served for something I didn't do, and I wouldn't testify to matters I had no knowledge of. Also, that with or without him I was going to trust God, knowing that He will deliver me at His appointed time.

On August 27, 2001, the six of us went to trial before a 12-panel jury. All odds were against us, but I knew God was with us. After the jury was picked, I suddenly felt scared and I began to waiver, but calmness instantly came over me when I began to recite to myself the 23rd Psalm.

The jury consisted of 11 whites and one black, plus one black alternate. On September 26, 2001, it took the jury less than 30 minutes to deliberate and come back with a Not Guilty verdict (see Appendix, p. 5, Doc. #3). The news of redemption came early on a Wednesday evening, carried down the block on the frantic legs of my daughter Rayven, who heard that her father was being released from lockup.

The federal jury had taken less than hour to reject the government's claims that I was a drug dealer–a dirty officer. I and five codefendants were acquitted in U.S. District Court in Ft. Lauderdale. After a trial that lasted nearly a month, the jury's stunningly quick verdict left me asking how a 15-year sheriff's deputy could have been accused and held in jail for more than a year on the word of paid informants and criminal snitches. I don't know how I went from being a highly decorated officer to an inmate overnight. Now I would try to leave prison and immediately become again father, husband, and free citizen.

I spent my first full day with my family since the Broward Sheriff's deputies stormed my home on June 15, 2000. I kept dwelling on the fact that they took another person's word over mine, and they incarcerated me for more than 16 months for a crime I didn't commit. Something's wrong with the system.

The charges were horribly painful, particularly for me. I've always been proud that I pulled myself out of poverty and was recognized for helping young offenders at the county jail. I knew people in all walks of life. And yet the U.S. attorney's office claimed I helped the twin brothers Barry and Bernard Smith run a major cocaine ring out of a warehouse around the corner from the Sheriff's Office (see Appendix, p. 6, Doc. #4). We all used that warehouse to lift weights and socialize; many of us were deputies, and some had been athletes, including myself, a star at Vero Beach High School who excelled in football, basketball, and track and later led my basketball team to District and Regional championships. In 1981, my team and I won the State Championship in football, and in track I still hold the record for the 440 dash, 440 relay, mile relay, mile medley relay, 880 relay, and the javelin throw. Until this day I am still recognized in my former high school's gymnasium for my athletic accomplishments.

Soon I received a full four-year scholarship at Missouri Southern State College. My freshman year I was runner-up for Rookie-of-the-Year, my sophomore year I broke all rushing records, and going into my junior year I was nominated for All-American. I left college in 1986,

I picked up my education later at Ashworth College in Georgia. I was able to maintain a 4.0 GPA while I attended, but the college wouldn't accept my credits from Missouri so I decided to withdraw. Later, with the encouragement of family and friends to follow my heart and intuition, I graduated with my bachelor's degree from American International University in 2011. Oh, my God, it gave me great joy to walk across that stage. I made the Dean's List in Criminal Justice/ Forensic Science and received a letter from the vice president of student affairs and associate provost at AIU for being one of the top students.

But before that, I was hired by the Broward Sheriff's Office, and played in the Pig Bowl 1987 through 1990 as a running back. The Pig Bowl was an annual charity game between the Sheriff's Office and other law-enforcement agencies. I was nominated MVP four times. In 1990 Sheriff Nick Navarro allowed me the opportunity to pursue my dreams and try out for the Miami Dolphins.

I was invited to the Dolphin camp by Mr. Charlie Winters, who was the director of player personnel. The try-out was unsuccessful, to my disappointment. I later tried out for the Orlando Predators of arena football, but after several weeks I cracked four ribs during practice and was placed on a waiver because the arena league kept a roster of only twenty-one players. I returned to B.S.O. but the following year I made a third attempt and tried out for the Professional Spring Football League. Sports have been an important and rewarding part of my life.

# Chapter Five

It was obvious from the beginning that there were problems in the case brought against me.

After a three-year investigation, including countless hours of surveillance video and 6,000 wire-tapped phone calls, the government found no cocaine, no cash proceeds, and no mention of drugs. The jury, which began listening to the case August 29 and began to deliberate about 4 p.m. that Wednesday, surprised US District Court Norman Roettger, the attorneys and the defendants by coming out with a verdict in less than an hour.

I responded to a question from a reporter: "Bitter? No, I'm not bitter, even though I have been declared a danger to the community, locked up for months, and denied bail twice."

The nearly all-white jury listened to the case against six black men and saw the truth, reaffirming my faith in human beings and my strong belief in God. I thank God for every one of those jurors. If I could hug and kiss every one of them, I would.

On September 26, 2001, bells kept ringing in the back of my mind when six jurors interviewed by the Sun-Sentinel declared they saw no evidence during the trial that should cost me my job. The Sheriff's Office released a report of their internal investigation detailing the reasons for firing me. Captain Keith Neely accused me of associating with criminals, lying to superiors, and transporting cocaine, a charge that the prosecutor had backed off from by the time of trial. Neely also stated that my off-duty activities impacted negatively upon the Broward Sheriff's Office operations. My lawyer and I say the report is a bogus means to a predetermined end. My attorney stated, "What they're doing is just trying to find a basis to try to fire this guy."

I suffered humiliation and the loss of my law-enforcement career, as well as losing my freedom and the companionship of my family. I had to bear the knowledge of the effects on my wife and two young daughters. There was my inability to care for and support them, not to mention the extreme financial burdens resulting from the cost of my defense and helplessness to earn a living. My wife, Patrice, a veteran of the U.S Postal Service, had to borrow money from family and friends to stay afloat. My mother could no longer pay for her 1997 Trans-Am convertible and had to give it up. Students taunted my 14-year-old daughter, Martrice.

And this saga came about because my former department failed to supervise the deputies' investigation and conduct, or to exercise even the most rudimentary review of the information allegedly obtained from informants and placed in the record by deputies, which turned out to be false. The investigative file, as well as testimony from the supervising sergeants, showed during trial that the "hands-off" supervisory practice reflected the policy that the sergeants were not required to exercise any actual supervision at all, but only to check the detectives' investigative reports for neatness!

What is really sad about this ordeal is that there was evidence that B.S.O. exercised no supervision of the confidential informants upon whose information they relied. As an end result, false information was presented to the federal authorities in their joint "Operation Home Team" investigation, as well as to the federal grand jury which ultimately issued a sealed indictment based on information that proved to be false.

I grew up in a poor part of the country and I was totally aware of poverty. My father and mother were migrant workers making a dollar an hour packing fruit, forced to drop out of school and harvest in the cotton fields of Georgia at the age of seven. My brother, sister, and myself were deprived of the joys of Christmas, Thanksgiving, and all the other important holidays we never experienced.

Those holidays were just normal days to my family. My parents didn't have sufficient finances to provide us with decent clothing for school. Our clothes came from World Thrift, but that never stopped us from achieving the goals we set out to achieve. I graduated from high school and went on to attend college, my sister graduated from high school, and we celebrated when my brother received his GED along with my 55-year-old mother. Even though life was hard, we were a motivated family.

I have tried to keep the flame of motivation alive in my children. My daughter Martrice excelled at Florida Atlantic University, winning the Honor America Society Award and graduating *summa cum laude*. Her sister, Rayven, is an honor roll student at Florida A&M University. Raymond Jr. is an honor roll student at Bair Middle School. I tell them I know this requires smart study skills, perseverance, hard work and dedication. When I was wrongfully incarcerated, other students taunted them in school, saying "You guys have that big house and expensive cars because your daddy is a drug dealer." I told them, "Your mom and I work extremely hard, we put our money together as one, and we have great credit, so why shouldn't our family be able to live a comfortable life?"

I remind them not to focus on the negative things people say; my mother always said that when you point your index finger and raise your thumb, the other three fingers are pointing back at you. "Strive to be the best that you can be, always put God first, and give 110 percent at whatever you attempt to do, and if for some reason you fall short, remember tomorrow is another day and that your mom and dad love you."

Parents often wonder why their children become associated with criminal activities and engage in criminal mischief. Well, think about it. Working parents never find the opportunity to spend quality time with their children because of their work schedules, including overtime, so their kids venture out to find a place of comfort. People seek those things that make them feel comfortable, whether it's drinking, smoking, weight-lifting, praying, or whatever.

When I was growing up, there was strife in our home. My father and mother constantly fought. Violence, sometimes stabbing, cutting and shooting, took place almost every Friday and Saturday and sometimes Sunday nights. My mother was shot by my father after a very big fight. There were many nights when my sister, brother, mother and I were forced out of the little house after my father came home from a late night out drinking and smoking marijuana and ready for a quarrel.

I hated the weekends because Friday, Saturday and some Sunday nights trouble would start as soon as my father walked through the door. I could never fall asleep on these nights because I was anticipating my father kicking the door to get in. I truly thanked God for the 4x4 horseshoe hinges that secured the door. I remember when I was twelve years of age and my father was getting ready to go out to party. Before he left the house he and my mother engaged in a physical altercation in which my mother sustained two black eyes and a bloodied mouth, her white gown ruined, with blood all over it. I wanted to help her but I was afraid of my father.

My mom grabbed me and said "Raymond, don't cry, everything's going to be all right." My father came home around 3 a.m. and fell asleep on the sofa. That's when my mother took her straight razor and began striking my father over his entire body. I saw his flesh open up; he must have thought it was a mosquito biting him because he would hit that area, striking out in his sleep.

I said to my mother, Bernice, "Don't cut him again," and she responded, "That bastard better be glad you're here because I would have killed him!"

My father hated the cops and had so many run-ins with the law that he finally came to the conclusion that he wanted to kill one. I protested, "Daddy the police are good people." His reply was, "They are very corrupt and cruel."

That statement inspired me to go to college and major in criminal justice and prove to my father that not every cop is bad. And yet what my father said to me seemed to turn out to be true because after 15 years of service, I was a victim of that very corruption. This happened after I spoke out about the officers who were involved in the pyramid scheme, planting drugs on innocent offenders, taking their money, and keeping it for their own self-gain. The Broward Sheriff's Office was manufacturing their own cocaine and giving it to us to sell as undercover deputies–and they kept the proceeds.

I remember working for the drug task force, the OCD, in a cradle operation, our word for an undercover operation conducted within 1,000 feet of a school. The purpose was to catch a person selling drugs near a school, for which they would receive a maximum of three years in the state penitentiary if proven guilty in the court of law. My colleagues and I would be given several cocaine rocks by our supervisor, and we'd conduct a sweep, taking all the drug dealers off the streets, arresting them and replacing them with undercover officers.

In some locations, undercover officers were selling the rocks for more than ten dollars. I witnessed officers turning in ten dollars and keeping the rest for themselves, sometimes leaving the street with thousands of dollars each night. I didn't just watch, I spoke up. "Guys, how could you do this? You're no better than the guys we just arrested."

They said, "Why don't you mind your own business and stay out of ours?"

"Look, you guys took an oath, you have an obligation to uphold the law. Instead, you're breaking the law."

It was from this office that the case against me was built. It was the result of a three-year investigation into a supposed cocaine ring that turned up no cocaine, no money, nor any mention of drugs in spite of more than

9,000 intercepted conversations and 138 surveillance videos. I told them from the beginning, "You have the wrong person. I'm going to keep fighting until I'm totally vindicated."

My mother faced the media. "My son worked since he was twelve years old, picking fruit, mowing lawns, and harvesting tobacco when I moved to Georgia for several years." I was a very talented athlete in high school, and it was then that I promised my mom that I would buy her a house when I turned pro, but I never quite made it after spending three years at Missouri Southern State College in Joplin, Missouri. I returned home and became a sheriff's deputy in 1986. I left the Sheriff's Office in 1991 for a brief and unsuccessful tryout with the Orlando Predators.

I became a fixture in the Corrections Departments Boot Camp Program and the voice of young offenders in the early 1990s. Although I have held many assignments, the most enjoyable for me have been those that involved working with troubled adolescents. My job was something that I took pride in. I tried to use my life as an illustration: If I did it, you can too. In 1999 I was awarded the Gold Cross Award, one of the highest Sheriff's Office honors, for subduing a gun-toting carjacker while unarmed and off duty (see Appendix, p. 10, Doc. #8).

I was named Deputy of the Month in July 1999 and March 1997 for other acts of bravery, including a jailhouse fight in which I broke both my hands and lost a knuckle coming to the defense of a sergeant (see Appendix, p. 11, Doc. #9). My 1997 firing was a result of hostile superiors, secretly unhappy that I spoke out about an illegal pyramid scheme that was going around the Sheriff's Office in 1996. The scandal resulted in the demotion of the B.S.O. union manager, the suspension of a deputy, and a dozen letters of reprimands.

I was out of work for eight months, working as a car salesman and an intern. An arbitrator found me guilty of very poor judgment but ruled I should be rehired, but without compensation. I returned to work September 15, 1998.

Until I was reinstated, I was employed at Al Hendrickson Toyota and at about this time started working out at Barry Smith's warehouse at 550 NW 27th Ave, where the Smith brothers ran a trucking business delivering Coca-Cola throughout the state. The warehouse was frequented by large men who liked to lift weights, including former NFL players such as Lorenzo White and Sterling Palmer. I fit right in; no one was more imposing than I was at 6 feet 1 inch and 285 pounds, and I could bench-press 500 pounds. Defense attorneys said investigators wanted to score a big public relations splash by indicting pro athletes, but neither White nor Palmer was ever charged.

The Smith warehouse provided me a chance to work out for free and hang out with people I had known from the neighborhood, which I visited during the summer as a child. Barry Smith admitted to the investigators that he once dealt drugs, and admitted during trial that he was in the business of brokering stolen cars.

I knew none of this, and my association was based largely on weight-lifting. I was unemployed for much of 1998; I would borrow $30 here, $20 there from Barry Smith. I eventually bought the 1993 Mercedes 400 SEL for $37,000 from Car Corps Incorporated, previously owned by Barry Smith, a deal that would arouse the suspicion of the sheriff's detective who didn't think a deputy sheriff making $47,000 a year could afford that class of car. Several members from the Drug Task Force wondered aloud how I could afford it, theorizing, "He must be selling drugs." It was none of their business, of course, but the fact was we were a two-income family, and our lives were no more lavish and no more frugal than other families we knew.

I filed a complaint to Internal Affairs because of the accusations floating around me, but the complaint went nowhere. In fact, I think it led to my own downfall. My attorney agreed, saying, "There's no doubt in my mind that this is what started the whole thing."

# Chapter Six

Operation Home Team, the operation that would sweep me up into its machinations, came about in 1997, when Ansell Pratt, a confidential sheriff's office source, reported that the twin Smith brothers were sizable drug dealers. This confidential source received $20,430 for expenses during that time and $15,880 in cash. On October 8, 1998, the Sheriff's Office raided the Smith warehouse and found no one there. The source said Barry Smith bragged that he was warned of the sweep, leading the source to think that Smith had his own source within the Sheriff's Office– the logical choice, me.

This source testified at trial that on November 4, 1998, "Raymond Hicks was at the warehouse most of the day and was given a paper bag by Barry Smith containing a kilo of cocaine." Richard Pisanti, who was B.S.O.'s investigator at that point, admitted that he never checked out that information. Had he done so, he would have learned that it couldn't be true, because I was at work on that day on the sixth floor of the Broward County jail as borne out by my work schedule (see Appendix, pp. 7-9, Docs. #5-7). If the sergeant had testified that he found out that I was in fact working that day, it would have cast doubt on the whole of the confidential source's information, but the sergeant signed off on the report without asking any questions.

The B.S.O. officers who worked with informant Ansel Pratt or relied on his alleged information all claimed not to know that several months prior to my arrest, Pratt was himself arrested by B.S.O. deputies for aggravated assault with a firearm, and that during the assault he had threatened to arrest the victim because he was a law-enforcement officer (see Appendix, p. 12, Doc. #10). All of the investigators mentioned in this case stated that had they known of that arrest, it would have affected their opinion as to Pratt's credibility and their decision to rely on the information provided by the informant. On May 22, 1999, the source reported that Barry Smith waved an envelope of documents and said I had "given him some good information." But plainly the source's information wasn't always right. In his most glaring error of judgment, he saw a duffel bag and reported that it was filled with cocaine when in fact it was a vacuum cleaner. "One of the jurors said everything this guy said was a lie," said Howard Nirenberd later.

The jurors were contacted by South Florida's Sun-Sentinel. After a month-long trial that contained mountains of evidence, the jury returned in 30 minutes but one juror told the newspaper, "We could have been back in 10." Another juror said, "What we could not believe was that so much money was spent and there was nothing concrete at the end." The jurors told the Sun-Sentinel they were shocked when I got up to testify and they saw that I along with my codefendants was in handcuffs and shackles. "You realized these guys had been in jail for more than 16 months." It was pretty sad, said Nirenberd, another juror. "I was pretty embarrassed, because I'm part of the system."

By the end of the trial, the charge that I had provided inside information to the Smith brothers had been reduced to ashes. The most compelling evidence of a connection surfaced in an F.B.I. recording of Bernard Smith asking sheriff's detective Bernard Brown, a long-time friend, if he could find out why officers were looking for the Smith brothers. Patrick Smith said he also asked favors of deputies Rudolph Nesbitt and Crystal Lewis. All were cleared after an internal sheriff's office investigation according to the sheriff's office documents.

I know that life for my wife and two daughters was made difficult. At the time of my arrest my wife had gone to the grocery store (the local Winn Dixie), like any other day. When I saw her again, I was in handcuffs and the Broward Sheriff's officers were everywhere. So were our neighbors. My wife was asking, "What's going on," over and over, but getting no answers. My wife had no idea what was going on or where they would be taking me. She found out hours later that I was being taken to Miami's federal detention center. She and the girls would be allowed to visit one day a week, for one hour, Saturdays only, four times a month. If there was a fifth Saturday in a month, it didn't count–there was no fifth visit.

They would come early on Saturday, since visitation started at 6 a.m., and stand in the dark across the street (rain or shine) with other families waiting to visit their loved ones. For sixteen and a half months they never missed a visit. It was the only time that we could actually see each other, visit and talk. It helped all of us to have that hour and we looked forward to every visit. Between visits, I'd call to make sure they were all right.

My wife, Patrice, assured me that she made every attempt to keep the girls' lives as normal as possible. She took them to cheerleading practice every day and if they had a Saturday game after our visit they went there as well. I know that working and taking care of the family was difficult without me there to help. My wife said from the beginning, "Raymond, I know all these things that you have been accused of are not true. We've been together too long for me to think that. I know you, and you're not that type of person." At trial she told me how nervous she was, because she had never had to testify before, had never had that public forum. I could see that she was rattled, but she was strong, She told me later that she'd had a panic attack after she finished answering the questions from both attorneys.

After being exonerated and released from court

I tried getting assistance (food stamps) from the government, but my request was denied. I went and filled out an application for unemployment and I was informed by one of the counselors that I was not eligible for unemployment compensation due to the fact that I had not worked within the last two years (have you tried to hold down a job while you are locked up in jail?).

On June 3, 2003, I applied for the position as a laborer for Astaldi Construction Company making nine dollars an hour and working thirteen hours a day. And I found myself in a situation I could not have imagined beforehand: a gentleman whom I'd helped with his case while being incarcerated in 1990 became my foreman on a construction site! My job consisted of me and my colleagues putting in sewer laterals and new water services. My fourteen years of education and fifteen years of service in law enforcement counted for nothing. I had to set my priorities to the side and get out there and provide for myself and my family.

I was ridiculed by several guys on the construction site because they had known me as an officer but now they saw me as a laborer. What made me continue to press on was my faith in God. I was encouraged by a statement made by a former federal prisoner who worked for the same company and who knew about my incarceration and also my verdict. He said to me, "Man, I know a lot of people are talking about you, but be strong and keep your head up."

On September 5, 2003, I submitted my resignation to Astaldi and accepted the job of first sergeant for the Elite Military Academy's program, "Boot Camp Drill Instructor." Later, my name was sent to Mr. Jim Moran for the African American Achievers' Award by the cadets in Boot Camp. In March 2004, I won this prestigious award (see Appendix p. 13, Doc. #11).

On October 9, 2003, my settlement and release agreement was entered into by and between Kenneth C. Jenne II, Sheriff of Broward County, and Raymond Hicks. Upon execution of this agreement, my termination of employment from the Broward Sheriff's Office was rescinded and B.S.O. simultaneously accepted this agreement as my final and irrevocable resignation from employment with that office (see Appendix p. 14, Doc. #12). I was informed that I was not eligible for reemployment and any future application for reemployment could be rejected based upon the terms of this agreement. Within ten days of this execution of the agreement, B.S.O. paid me a one-time lump-sum payment of $100,000 made payable to the trust accounts of my lawyer Bruce Little, P.A.

Vindication, indeed.

We had little respite from our troubles, however. On January 6, 2004, my wife and I came home after being in court regarding a lawsuit about our car, and found our home surrounded by B.S.O. deputies as the harassment and retaliation continued. The Broward

Sheriff's officers stormed my residence (again), detaining me and alleging that they had received a 911 report that I was shooting in the back of my home (see Appendix, p. 15 Doc. #13). I informed them that I had just that minute arrived at home from court, so how could I have been the shooter?

One of the deputies placed me in handcuffs (again) and told me that they were going to hold me until their investigation was completed. Prior to their placing me in handcuffs I asked if I could call my attorney and the deputy replied sarcastically, "Go right ahead." I reached Mrs. Nancy at Mr. Little's office and I informed her that fifty patrol cars and officers had stormed my residence. She assured me she would let Mr. Little know.

It was stated to me by a deputy that the person working at the Citgo called 911 and said I was shooting at someone, and the shots were coming in the direction of his store. My home was taped off and 44th Street was taped off as well. I was standing there in handcuffs. Again. I asked the deputies if they could loosen the handcuffs because they were too tight. The deputy responded, "You'll be all right." Note: I have taken pictures of the physical marks the handcuffs left (see Appendix, p. 16, Doc. #14). And through it all, I kept informing the deputies, "You guys are wrong." Speaking with a sergeant, I asked him to "go and get your so-called witness and have him identify me." They declined to go and get this person. So I asked the sergeant, "Why would all of you guys come in force straight to my home and detain me?" He said again that the tenant at the Citgo gas station called 911 and identified me as the shooter. I said flat-out, "Man you're lying. No one told you that. You guys are here because of my pending case against B.S.O."

Between six o'clock and seven, one of the other deputies stated to me that he was going to release me and take a picture of me (that never took place). A tall white gentleman showed up in my yard. He must have been a lieutenant or captain. I asked my wife to go without delay and show him the documents showing that we had just come from court. Within seconds after he finished reading the order from the judge, all fifty officers dispersed.

After they released me, I went to the Citgo and asked the tenant if he had called 911 and he said yes. He informed me that a black male ran up to his window and said someone is shooting, can you please call 911, and that was when he reported the shooting to communications. After I informed him of what they said about his saying I was the shooter, he got very angry and called 911 again and asked the communications operator why she would lie about him.

During the investigation, one of the sergeants and another deputy searched inside my home without a search warrant or probable cause. There were no bullet casings, and they didn't check for gunpowder.

I had just received a prestigious award from the J.M. Foundation nominating me for the African American Achievers Award on March 11 2004. On March 25, I had to appear in court for discharging a firearm in public. The state prosecutor asked the judge for a continuance, the judge denied his request, so we proceeded with trial. Thirty minutes, later in case #04000243MM20A, I was acquitted by the court.

As the harassment continued, on October 10, 2005, I was arrested again, this time for child abuse after a female cadet ran away from home and was paddled by a female major, even though I did not participate (see Appendix, p. 17, Doc. #15). I have three beautiful children of my own (a son was born after most of the events in this book took place), and I love children. I'm the last person anyone should accuse of child abuse.

I was looking down the barrel of the Broward Sheriff's deputies' guns with their finger on the trigger as they eagerly waited for the opportunity to take my life. Each time I've been arrested, my attorney has taken depositions from the officers who were involved in my case, but, hysterically enough, they never remember anything pertaining to my case. All of these individuals have been promoted to commanders, captains and sergeants. On May 12, 2006, my attorney was asked by the state attorney to send her a letter containing a summary of some of the reasons why he believed the pending charges against me should be dropped. One of his reasons: According to the alleged victim, "[Mr. Hicks] was supportive, gave her motivational materials and gave her reason to feel better about herself, and she has not had the same self-respect since leaving the school where he worked. According to the alleged victim, her time at Elite Academy was a good and productive time in her life and she saw the benefit that that type of discipline could produce."

The administrator of the school, who perhaps was the most credible of the witnesses deposed so far and who had a graduate degree in education and had been the assistant dean of students at the University of Arkansas, reported that the cadets loved me and that I was warm and engaging and it was obvious that I loved the kids as well. According to the administrator, she received a call from child protective services clearing me of any wrongdoing and was advised that I could return to the school.

The Miami Herald reported, "[Mr. Hicks has] dedicated his life to helping young adults become responsible members of their communities. He is highly regarded by the young cadets. The cadets describe him as someone who takes time to listen, to tell it like it is, and is firm and caring. The students said that he has turned their lives around." For some unknown reason, this case was not filed until one and a half years after the alleged abuse. My attorney stated that if anyone views my alleged conduct in this case and considers my background in his judgment must conclude that this prosecution is ill-advised and unwarranted. He stated. "I've known Ray personally for years and am familiar with his commitment to help children. I know that he is the last person on earth who would ever do anything to physically harm a child and I implore you to drop these charges."

All charges were dropped by the state attorney on August 14, 2006.

After several letters making contact with the Florida Department of Law Enforcement, the Federal Bureau of Investigation, the state government office, the inspector general's office and also the civil rights division out of Washington, D.C., the offices mentioned here conducted a thorough investigation within the Broward Sheriff's Office. The outcome of the investigation:

Twenty-nine officers faced felony counts for falsifying documentation. Seven of those officers were found guilty of misconduct and are now serving time within the penal system. On September 6, 2007, an article in The Sun-Sentinel stated "Ex-sheriff tells court he's guilty and apologizes for errors in his judgment." The sheriff left federal court on Wednesday barred from voting or holding public office, unable to own a gun and required to submit to random urine tests. It was a humiliating moment when he pled guilty on federal mail fraud and income tax evasion. And then he faced 18 to 20 months in prison.

On November 17, 2007, at sentencing, Sheriff Jenne began to weep. He was ordered to pay $3,000 in fines and would be on supervised release, similar to probation, for another year after he was freed. He also had to serve a year and a day in federal prison. A United States attorney stated, "He should be locked up for two years." He felt a tougher sentence would have been more appropriate for a high-ranking public official who misused his office and breached the public trust. The federal investigation of Jenne began when the Broward State Attorney's Office uncovered irregularities in Jenne's finances while state prosecutors were investigating a false confessions scandal and the manipulation of crime statistics by the Sheriff's Office.

Then Governor Jeb Bush ordered the Florida Department of Law Enforcement to take over the investigation because State Attorney Mike Satz was once a close friend of Jenne's. Federal prosecutors joined the investigation two years ago. Jenne admitted he accepted more than $151,625 in improper payments, income and other benefits from Sheriff's Office contractors, including money funneled through his secretaries and payments on a Mercedes convertible from his former law firm, Conrad, Scherer and Jenne. "He was supposed to be an example to the deputies he led and the residents of Broward County."

# Chapter Seven

Below is the document we filed before the civil trial began, just one more example of the obstruction and behind-the-scenes manipulation of the case (see also Appendix, pp. 18-20, Doc. #16).

PLAINTIFF'S SWORN MOTION TO DISQUALIFY

Comes now, the plaintiff, Raymond Hicks, by and through his undersigned counsel pursuant to Rule 2.330 Florida Judicial Administration Rule and Florida Statue 38.10 (2007), and herein moves to disqualify the Trial Judge in this case, Barry E. Goldstein, and as grounds therefore would show:

1. In preparation for trial on this case undersigned was advised by a fellow attorney on April 4, 2008, that the possibility existed that the trial judge, Judge Barry E. Goldstein, has a brother who is a high-ranking official in the Broward County Sheriff's Office. The undersigned has no prior knowledge of this, nor had it been disclosed by the Court or opposing counsel.

2. This case involves substantial issues with regard to credibility of certain members of B.S.O. as well as legal issues raised with the Court on the liability of members of the Broward County Sheriff's Office with regard to the issues raised by the plaintiff.

3. Immediately upon learning this information, the undersigned undertook an investigation to determine whether in fact the information was correct and although it could not be actually verified, it was determined that there was an individual by the name of Michael Goldstein who is a major with the Broward County Sheriff's Office who is rumored to be related to Judge Barry E. Goldstein. That person has held positions in Road Patrol and in Human Resources during the time period covered by the facts in this case.

4. By his signature affixed hereto, Raymond Hicks fears that he will not receive a fair trial or hearing because of a potential prejudice or bias of the Judge as the Judge is related to an individual who has close ties with the Broward County Sheriff's Office and maybe in the chain of command of the individuals who will testify in this case and whose credibility will be questioned.

5. After beginning the investigation on this matter, the undersigned contacted counsel for the Broward County Sheriff's Office who verified that Michael Goldstein was a major until the recent past with the Broward County Sheriff's Office, and he in fact is the brother of Barry E. Goldstein the Judge."

I had never given up on finding documents vital to my lawsuit. Sure enough, on July 25, 2008, a newspaper article alerted me to missing documents that had turned up. It reported, "B.S.O. is not providing any explanations, but a tape recording of a wired-tapped phone conversation and other documents that are being described as key evidence in a lawsuit filed against the agency have now surfaced after more than eight years." (see Appendix, pp. 2-4, Doc. #2)

I was praying in my bathroom as I do every day when the spirit of the Lord spoke to me and said, " When you finish praying, don't tell your attorney but go down to Internal Affairs and you will receive the tape and documents you've been trying to get for the last eight years." I arrived at I.A., paid $111 and received everything mentioned above. Despite countless public requests over the past eight years, B.S.O. had told me and my attorney they "couldn't find it." My attorney had issued subpoenas to get copies of the records and filed numerous pleas seeking to have the court issue an order that would force B.S.O. to hand them over.

In response to an April 2006 motion to compel, B.S.O. submitted a sworn affidavit from Internal Affairs and Commander Joseph Fitzpatrick. The Commander stated that Internal Affairs as well as the records division and risk management office had searched for the tape recording that was the subject of plaintiff's April 5, 2006, motion to compel and subsequent orders. This affidavit was filed with the court on February 22, 2007, and stated: "The Broward Sheriff's Office has not located the tape and is not presently in possession, custody, or control of the tape."(see Appendix, pp. 21-22, Doc. #17) The affidavit further affirmed, "The tape is a recording of a

July 23, 1999, wired-tapped conversation that took place between Bernard Smith, one of the five codefendants along with Hicks, in the federal drug trafficking case, and then B.S.O. deputy Bernard Brown III, who is now a detective in the department, Hicks having been accused of providing confidential department information to the codefendants."

During the federal trial it was learned it was actually Brown and not me who is heard during the conversation. How I was named as being ID'd on this tape is still a mystery to me, unless it was part of a general effort to discredit me and my criticism of the Office–by any means. The tape in question details how Smith, who was under investigation for drug trafficking at the time, made a call to Brown seeking information on the case. Brown can be heard in a profanity-laced phone conversation, replete with racial slurs, agreeing to assist Smith in determining what B.S.O. investigators were after when they came looking for one of Smith's brothers. Brown asked Smith for descriptions of the deputies and suggested they may have been from the fugitive squad, indicating it may have been a possible child-support matter. "Was it that real big cracker?" Brown questioned. After explaining the uniforms they wore might not identify the unit they were from, he agreed to check into it.

"What I can do is, tonight while I'm at work I

can have one of my girls run his name," the voice, now confirmed to be that of Brown, responded. Brown went on to ask Smith for his brother's name and date of birth, of which Smith said he wasn't sure, but agreed to call Brown right back with that information. At trial, and while undergoing questioning by the federal prosecutor, Smith testified that several B.S.O. employees had in fact done favors for him, but he had only asked Brown to run checks on the drivers' licenses of family members, nothing more.

Smith denied on the stand that Hicks had done any favors for him. "I don't get personal favors from Raymond Hicks. All me and Raymond Hicks ever did was spot each other for weights," Smith testified. During further questioning from the prosecutor, Smith was asked to identify the law-enforcement officials who did favors for him. "Bernard Brown. But I don't recall any Raymond Hicks asking no favors like that," he testified. Following the trial, Fitzpatrick conducted an Internal Affairs investigation into Smith's allegations against Brown. During questioning by Fitzpatrick, Brown acknowledged it was he who is heard on the wiretapped phone conversations agreeing to get information for Smith. "That was in the middle of the day, and I was asleep and umm, I think at the time I was working at night, you know, on midnight shift, and I don't remember contacting anybody for that information." Brown went on to explain that he and Smith grew up in the same Central Broward neighborhood, and that their parents were from the same town in Georgia. Despite the tape recording detailing the conversation and the testimony from the trial, Brown was cleared of any wrongdoing, as described in a May 17, 2002, final report where the allegations were determined to be unfounded. Brown remains with the department and has been promoted to detective.

Meanwhile, I'm desperately praying and asking someone–anyone–to investigate the corruption and misconduct that lies buried in the Broward Sheriff's Office and also the 17th Judicial Court System in Broward County, Florida. Attached to this memoir you will find a copy of the plaintiff's motion for the relief of judgment and incorporated memorandum of law. In paragraph two it states "This action in appointing a retired judge to hear the case would have been accomplished pursuant to administrative order 1-92-1-1 of the 17th Judicial Circuit, in and for Broward County, Florida." (see Appendix, pp. 23-28, Doc. #18)

It further states that at the beginning of trial, both counsels inquired of Judge Breger as to his legal authority to hear the case based upon the fact that he was a retired County Court Judge from Dade County, Florida.

Judge Breger advised the parties' counsels that there was a Supreme Court order allowing him to hear the case as a retired County Court Judge. The trial commenced and eventually resulted in a final judgment rendered by the court on May 23, 2009.

My attorney, Bruce Little, attempted to find the order allowing Judge Breger to hear the case and ultimately determined that no such order was ever issued. On May 28, 2009, my attorney received an e-mail from the General Counsel from the Broward Sheriff's Office of the 17th Judicial Circuit, attaching an Administrative Order allegedly rendered by the court on May 28, 2009, nunc pro tunc to May 11, 2009. (A court ruling nunc pro tunc, "now for then," is applied retroactively to correct an earlier ruling) (see Appendix, pp. 29-30, Doc. #19-20).

The essence of the order allegedly appointed Honorable Eli Breger as senior judge for temporary duty to the Circuit Court and in and for the 17th Judicial Circuit to hear the case of Raymond Hicks vs. B.S.O. et al.

It is the plaintiff's position herein that the order rendered by the court on May 28, 2009, nunc pro tunc to May 11, 2009, ineffectively attempted to vest Judge Breger with jurisdiction retroactively and as such the final judgment rendered by Judge Breger is void. I can only conclude that this is a direct violation of my rights under the Fifth and also the Sixth Amendments.

When on May 11, 2009, the civil trial between

me and B.S.O. commenced, defending attorney Mike Piper submitted several motions to the court. On Count 1, Malicious Prosecution, Judge Breger ruled, "The defendants' motion is hereby denied." Mr. Piper became very upset and stated to Judge Breger in a loud tone of voice, "I will appeal." The Judge responded, "My ruling is final."

There were other motions heard, some in my favor and some in the defendants'. On May 18, 2009, court commenced at 9:30 a.m. Judge Breger informed the court that over the course of the weekend he had received a package Fed Ex'd overnight to his residence from the defendant's attorney, Mike Piper (Bar #710105). Judge Breger further stated, "Inside the package was a transcript." He thanked Mr. Piper for sending it and stated that he had read the entire transcript.

Mr. Piper refused to allow my attorney Bruce Little (Bar #284580) to review the documents contained in the package. According to a civil case 8:07-CV-00308-T-23MSS dated August 7, a motion was filed by the plaintiff for Procedural Misconduct stating that the defendants' action without sending a copy to the plaintiff was in violation of federal rules of civil procedures.

Mr. Piper intentionally sent the package to the Judge's residence to prejudice this case. Mr. Piper knew based upon the testimony we'd heard so far that Broward Sheriff's Office was losing their case. During the course of the trial, some of the jurors were openly wiping their eyes as they listened to the witnesses testify in my favor. Judge Breger had also allowed jurors to ask questions of the witnesses during the trial, which generally strengthened my case. Things were looking up for our side, and we were in good spirits. I'd won the criminal trial–I was no criminal, and the evidence showed that. The civil case, we thought, should be a slam-dunk.

It was after he received the overnight Fed Ex documents that the judge began to wind up the trial. Judge Breger asked both counsels if they had anything to say before he gave his ruling on all counts.

Then Judge Breger gave the defendant a directed verdict.

In a directed verdict, the decision is taken out of the hands of the jury by the judge. There is no longer any need for the jury to decide the case. A judge generally takes this course when he concludes that no reasonable jury could reach a decision to the contrary. Did the documents delivered to his home (which we were not allowed to see) convince him of that?

Would we ever know the answer?

In closing my account of these painful years, I'd like to say that I know for a fact that attorney Mike Piper did not want this case to go before the jury for deliberation. After Judge Breger gave a directed verdict, the jurors were called back into the courtroom. The Judge thanked them for coming, issued them a certificate and dismissed them.

As the jurors walked out of the courtroom, several said to me and my family, "God bless you" and "I wish you the best."

I don't understand how the judge could rule in favor of the defendant when my rights were violated on false arrest and imprisonment as well as malicious prosecution as a result of B.S.O.'s lax supervisory policy; I had a good case for action for false arrest. I presented sufficient evidence to support those claims at my civil trial. In my opinion the trial court judge clearly made a mistake in directing a verdict against me at the close of my case, because if the evidence were properly accepted as true, and if all reasonable inferences were drawn in my favor and evidentiary conflicts resolved in my favor as well, a jury could as well also be presented with the overriding issue of lack of probable cause. As a result of the directed verdict, I was subjected to a further deprivation of my rights, when what I was expecting this time was that my rights would be restored against the entity responsible for my wrongful arrest, false imprisonment, and prosecution.

As my family and I left the courtroom in stunned disbelief after the Judge's abrupt decision, we bumped into Mr. Piper who began laughing at our grim faces in an unprofessional manner. I advised Mr. Piper that the case was not over yet. There was sufficient evidence supporting the claims discussed above to warrant their consideration by a jury. The judge who tried this case did not explain or discuss his ruling, so I had to assume that he found no jury issues as to any of the causes of actions, including the section 1983 count. But granting B.S.O.'s motion for a directed verdict was clearly a mistake. I was deprived of my Fourth and Fourteenth Amendment rights because of B.S.O. policies. I ask and pray every chance I get that someone will please investigate this matter.

In the middle of all this, on July 31, 2009, I won a lifesaving award for coming to the aid of a detainee who tried to kill himself after the judge read him his charges in court (see Appendix, p. 31, Doc. #21).

I like to think that this is the real Ray Hicks, not the shackled man in the courtroom in the criminal trial.

While I am presently working for the United States Department of Homeland Security, Immigration, Custom and Enforcement with a company by the name of Doyon Akal Security, which is subcontracted through the federal government, my family and I continue to suffer because of the corruption, dishonesty and unprofessional behavior displayed by the Broward Sheriff's Office and the court system in Broward County, Florida. This entire ordeal, for the past nine years, has become an agonizing nightmare.

# Chapter Eight

This is what the power of prayer and positive thinking can do for you.

There is a direct link between believing in what you pray for and receiving it. God is sovereign in human affairs, but that does not relieve us of our responsibility. We must ask the Lord to show us what He wants our life's work to be. Then we must trust Him to direct and guide our actions and affirmations. If we have faith in God and in ourselves He will provide us with a place of refuge and strength. Prayer is my spiritual being manifesting in a physical dimension.

Prayer and positive thinking provide strength when alone and when we tend to give up in a situation or on a person who seems helpless. Healing is another power that is sought after through prayer. Oftentimes we ask God for forgiveness for our imperfect selves and the wrongdoings we stumble into daily. Probably most importantly we should remember to give thanks in our prayers and ask God to guide others in need, especially those who are our enemies and who need the most assistance.

Effective prayer can be practiced and attained through silent meditation in which one can prayeritize, picturize, and actualize. Create in the form of prayer what it is you seek to have happen. Talk it over with God in a natural manner as if God were right there with you. Visualize a detailed image that can be seen clearly when you close your eyes. Then actually imagine the prayer and picture it becoming reality. Repeat this process with a clear mind free of worries and problems so as to concentrate on the desired results. Then believe that you are in God's hands and truly accept that all things asked in prayer, if they are God's will, will happen.

Another method in communicating prayer is in the form of a song. It is uplifting and creative to rejoice in song, offering your heart to God's will, sending vibrations in unison with others. A simple but effective form of prayer is to verbalize out loud in words, in your own language, focusing all forces positively, never using negative thoughts or words. At the end, say out loud, "God gives me the power to attain whatever I want and God will see me through all adversities."

To reach an understanding we must practice living with God, using His support and power. God will always answer our prayers. Sometimes He will say no, and sometimes He will say not yet. Prayer and positive thinking are not always as easy as they sound when dealing with situations that seem so unfair and that weigh so heavily on you. It's not a habit that you're born with, or that many people can achieve. I myself, although brought up in a holiness church, did not effectively understand this concept until recently.

Fifteen years ago I was called to a career that would change my daily life and the people in it. It was a career/a life that only those in fellowship will truly relate to. It's one that is more often than not filled with negativity, unfairness, suffering, fear and putting our lives on the line daily for those who have no regard for ours. It was at this point that I learned to put myself in God's hands and trust that His will be done. For the first time in my life, I asked God daily to protect me and my brothers and sisters, and then at the end of each day thanked him for the chance to do it again.

I experienced the effects of this powerful approach firsthand almost eight years ago when I was perceived as a mentor, someone of considerable size and strength–both inner and outer–and with a heart filled with concern for others first. Here's what happened: I was suddenly stricken with meningitis. I became very ill and was hospitalized. By the time people had the chance to visit me I had lost a considerable amount of weight, I had tubes attached to my nose, mouth and wrists and bore bruises on my backside from injections for pain which made it impossible for me to lie in comfort. I had just survived a painful spinal tap when the nurse announced that I had a visitor, my friend Lisa O'Brien, and advised me to rest instead, but I welcomed the company. I could only whisper but I said, "Glad to see you, love, how are you?"

I encouraged my friend to be strong and not to

worry about me. Should God spare my life, I'd be back soon. We prayed together and after our visit was up I told her to inform my co-workers and a group of 60 young men and women at Boot Camp that I was rehabilitating.

Lisa told me later that before entering the room where the students waited she took a moment to pray for the strength to convey my message. With a lump in her throat so big that she could barely speak, she saw them standing in line so silently you could hear a pin drop as she managed to gather herself. She told them that I was fighting for my life now, but "Don't worry, he'll be back soon." Without another word, one by one everyone joined hands and the young man who needed my help the most stepped forward and prayed out loud. Another young man asked if they could all write letters for her to bring to me. The next day she brought the letters and in a low voice I struggled (with tears in my eyes) to read each one out loud. A couple of days later everyone began to see the results of prayer and positive affirmations. I only hope that if someone else is faced with what I've been faced with, God will give him and her the strength to endure.

Attached you will find witness statements of those who were incarcerated with me. Also, the affidavits of my codefendants, stating that I never combined or conspired with them to commit any type of illegal act (see Appendix, pp. 32-37, Doc. # 22). That still wasn't good enough for the F.B. I. and the prosecutors to release me; they wanted to make an example out of me.

You will also find a letter from the U.S. Department of Justice Federal Bureau of Prisons, "To Whom It May Concern," a memorandum titled "Inmate Assistance during Medical Emergency", a notice of my second court date for discharging a firearm in public, my acquittal by the court, and a character reference from Ms. Lynda Brown, School Administrator of Elite Leadership Military Academy (see Appendix, pp. 38-42, Doc. # 23).

But before I write "The End" at the close of this account, I want to describe the day I came home.

On September 26, 2001, my family and friends had no idea it would be the last day of the trial; they left court early and returned home. One of my co-workers from the Sheriff's Office had stayed until the end of court, and he happened to hear the verdict being handed down by the foreman of the jury. He whispered to me, "Ray, I'm going to stick around and give you a ride home." I was struck with the joy of navigating the streets of Broward county as a free man and taking in the wonders of society as a full member of that society.

I knocked on my own front door and, knowing my wife would look through the peephole to check who was outside, I put my finger over it. She called out, "Who is it?" I didn't respond, and a minute later my wife and my two daughters were standing in the open door, radiant looks on their faces, tears flowing down their cheeks, holding prayer hands to their mouths in disbelief that I was really standing there. I was home! To this day I still feel chills when I think about that moment.

They rushed me and gave me the biggest hugs and kisses. I thought I was being hit by three linebackers, but it was a feeling I wouldn't trade for the world. My youngest daughter tells me that she had a premonition. She began to bang on the front-door window until her mother asked her what was wrong. "Daddy is coming home," she repeated, "Daddy is coming home." In spite of her doubts, her mom started cleaning the house.

There are times when I get goose bumps just remembering. When I walked through the door it seemed very strange to me. The suffering of being locked up is hard to leave behind. People free in the world tend to take the smallest things for granted, such as walking on green grass, breathing fresh air, coming and going as they please–these are some of the things I'd been craving. I carried my own inner wounds from my personal sense of suffering and loss.

I recall my first night lying in the comfort of my own king-size bed instead of the single cot at the detention center. I told my wife and kids how uncomfortable the steel bed felt. I told them that I spent many days and nights wondering if I would be able to spend time with my children, eating "real food" like macaroni and cheese, collard greens, fried chicken and homemade cornbread, surrounded by family and friends. I described to them what it was like to waken to hear "Count time. All inmates need to be out of bed and standing at the door," while the officer called your name and conducted a by-name, by-face headcount, what a lockdown is like, and how it feels being told by the officers what to do every single day.

I told them how the inmates, on the day they are to be released, rush to hear their names called. The unit becomes motionless, and nobody says a word. When the inmate's name is called, everyone says a silent prayer for the departing man, because there's a saying in the institution, "When the prayer goes up the blessing comes down." After the prayer the entire unit becomes united. It's a bizarre experience when you hear your own name broadcast. I told them about walking down this long hall with handcuffs on and shackles cutting into my ankles, impatient to reach the release desk. Some officers can feel your pain; however, there is always an officer who says, "See you soon," with a smirk on his face. I said to myself, *He is an idiot, he doesn't know me.* The marshal opened the door and I was a free man.

This is life throughout the United States in every federal detention center. The 365 days plus another 135 days I spent locked up felt like an eternity.

I told them I was treated like I was nothing but a

piece of rubbish the past two years of my life, and that there is nothing I wouldn't do to maintain my freedom. They tell me everything will be all right. My family will never know what I had to go through to reclaim my innocence. I tell them every day that it is truly a blessing from God to be home again.

The end

# Special Addendum

I have asked my daughters to write their memories of the day I was arrested and taken from our home. Here is the recollection of Martrice Hicks, who was 12 years old on that day:

Just another ordinary day outside with my dad as he lifted weights when officers jumped over the wall in the backyard of our house, raced around the corner of our residential entrance, and stormed my house. From their alarming tones and disgruntled expressions, I knew something was wrong. "Raymond Hicks, you have the right to remain silent" were the frightening words the armed men in uniforms belched, some with smug faces, half-smiling pure revenge, and others showing pity. I stood frozen in terror. "What are you doing and where are you taking my dad?" I asked as a deputy grabbed my father, but at the age of 12, I was easily ignored. Understand, I had no clue what was taking place as they raided my home with their iridescent flashing lights on their patrol cars, but it stung like a poisonous snakebite when I saw someone place handcuffs on my father's wrists; I began to cry. Belligerently I raced to the telephone to call my mother who had just gone to the store up the street. My body ached from a tormenting pain as if someone had just performed open-heart surgery while I watched, and then my mom finally arrived. Startled and confused, she jumped out of the car and raced toward my dad and me, and I thought maybe finally we could get some answers. During this turn of events, I was a part of a surreal nightmare that I needed to wake up from, but it would be long before I forgot this tragedy. Following up after my father's arrest, every television broadcast news station had something new to talk about as they paraded my father's picture and those of some other individuals all over the TV and newspaper. At school, the teasing continued on for days, and weeks. I often wondered how kids could be so cruel. They would say, "Your daddy is a drug dealer, that's how your family got that expensive house and nice cars." Ignorance is contagious because word spread around the entire school. We were all too young to understand the significance of what had taken place, but eventually I found myself in numerous conflicts that resulted in some fights; I was backed into a corner, and it was at that moment I realized I had no friends.

The following is the memory of my younger daughter, Rayven Hicks:

On June 15, only 8 years old, I was outside playing with my friends, and all of a sudden I see police cars everywhere. I looked down the street where my house was and noticed all the cars stopping in the front and back of the house, so I ran home. My cousin Shea who was living with us at the time was yelling, "They got Uncle Raymond!" When I finally get home I see my dad in the garage with handcuffs on. He tried to smile and turned around so I wouldn't see them. I had no idea what was going on, I opened the door and my sister was crying on the phone. I ran to the back of the house and there were more police. Nobody would tell me anything, I guess because I was so young. I ran to the front of the house and saw my mom crying. All the neighbors were standing outside just staring. I didn't know what to do or what was going on, so I started crying too. I saw the police put my dad in the backseat of a car and take him away. At the time I didn't think anything of it, I thought he was going to come right back. From that point on I would constantly ask my mom, "When is Daddy coming home?" Every Saturday from the time they took him away we would get up at 4 a.m. to go visit my dad at the federal detention center in Miami. Once we got there we had to wait in line outside for a long time and once we got into the building we still had to wait. I remember one Saturday, I had my hair done because I had a cheerleading competition, and the hair style I had required hairpins. The officers were so nasty to me as well as my mom and sister, they made me take down my hair, take off my shoes, belts, jewelry, etc. I became overjoyed when I saw my father coming through the door. Every Saturday, I'd ask him "Daddy, when are you coming home?" and his reply would always be, "Daddy will be home soon." When we left the detention center

I would always get teary-eyed because I didn't want to leave without him.

I'm including below a letter from my great friend Coreen Anderson. She is an incredible woman. When I was detained, Coreen told me, "Raymond, keep your head up because God has everything in control." Furthermore, she advised me that her church was praying for my deliverance. During the harassment that followed, she would always say, "Hon, I'm your friend, and I'm always here for you." Her mother, Mrs. Pelieta Fagan, who is my godmother and whom I also call "Mom," said the same, and backed me up all the way. Mom told me that I must forgive my colleagues, and reminded me, "You must forgive your brother and sister for the things they do wrong if you want God to forgive you your wrongdoing."

While I was incarcerated, Coreen said to me, "Raymond, I had a dream that you came home and I ran all the way down to your house and knocked on the door to congratulate you." Her dreams and prayers became a reality when I was released. I jogged one block to her home and knocked on the door. When the door opened, Coreen, her mother, Mrs. Pelieta Fagan, and Coreen's sister Margaret were standing there staring as if they were looking at a ghost. To show them my appreciation and love for having my back, as God continues to bless me I will always have their backs. Forever and a day.

February 25, 2013

On June 15, 2000, my life was significantly changed when Raymond Hicks was falsely arrested on fabricated charges of what appeared to be some monster trafficking of drugs to various states.. His picture was displayed on every local newscast and in the newspapers. At no time did I ever believe the allegations concocted by the Broward Sheriff's Office where he was employed and where he took great pride in his job. I knew there was more to the story.

I have known Raymond Hicks to be a very honest person and because he blew the whistle on his own agency they made every attempt to discredit him. As he remained in the federal detention center awaiting trial his family began to suffer physically, mentally, emotionally and financially. My family and I stepped in to assist his family the best way we could because we knew what type of person Raymond Hicks was and we knew without a shadow of a doubt that the allegations against Raymond Hicks were false and a tactic to silence his request for justice. It was a horror movie being played right before my eyes.

What I thought would be a few days in the federal detention center ended up being a grueling 16 ½ months in custody with the judge denying bond twice. But Raymond Hicks continued to fight for what he believed in.

These serious charges carried a life sentence and Raymond knew that this battle was no longer his but the Lord's. His faith was now on trial. I attended several hearings as the defense proved that the individual who was in custody should never have been there. The state did not prove its case. It was demonstrated that Raymond Hicks had never traveled to any of the states that were mentioned by the prosecution, he never had any involvement in illegal activities of any kind, and the state had no evidence of any drugs and no evidence linking him to selling drugs whatsoever! I asked myself, "How can you charge an innocent man with conspiracy to traffic 350 kilograms of cocaine and then during the trial you produce no drugs and no evidence?" I was completely ashamed of the criminal justice system.

On September 26, 2001, the truth prevailed and it took a jury of his peers less than a half hour to deliberate and come back with a Not Guilty verdict.

I have never met a man as strong as Raymond Hicks. His faith in God is remarkable. However, this incident has not gone without resulting hardships relating to the chain of events that would follow once he was exonerated. People tend to believe that once you are released from jail and found Not Guilty then the story is over, but not so.

Every day, I watched Raymond Hicks defend himself as he was denied Food Stamps, denied Unemployment Compensation, and lost his retirement funds. He applied for multiple jobs in the course of one year but due to his background check employers denied his application. He also had an enormous amount of attorney's fees to pay for a crime he did not commit.

I could see Broward Sheriff's Office patrol car and a white van with dark tinted windows parked behind his home every night in an effort to put fear in his heart. Broward Sheriff's Office continued the harassment by pulling him over a few days after he was released and issuing him a traffic ticket for his window tint being "too dark." The deputy laughed as he called his name, "Raymond Hicks," and made a mockery out of giving him the ticket. On another occasion, Raymond was arrested again for allegedly shooting at someone from his backyard. Ironically, at the time of the alleged shooting, Raymond was in the Broward County Courthouse more than 22 miles away on another matter. He took that case to court and was acquitted by the judge. It was just a joke to the agency as they continued to taunt him. Raymond also received a message on his home phone that stated, "You will be found in a pool of blood!" This message suspiciously could not be traced by Broward Sheriff's Office dispatch. How ironic! I could not believe that the very agency that patrolled and governed the Broward County area and the neighborhood where I live could be so corrupt.

As time went on, Raymond began to appeal his case. At that time, he began to complain of chest pains frequently and he had to be taken to the emergency room on several occasions for anxiety and depression, understandably, due to what he was still going through. I continued to encourage Raymond and pray with him and I provided him with a new Bible so that he could continue to read the work of God. I knew that the physical trial was over but the mental trial that he had to face would continue.

Many of the detectives for Broward Sheriff's Office who were directly involved in falsely arresting Raymond Hicks at his home in the presence of his family were promoted within the agency as if it was the Oscar awards they received for their best role in getting Raymond out of the agency. But Raymond continued to work through all adversities and in 2004 he won the African American Achievers Award that was sponsored by the Jim Moran Foundation for helping misdirected children change their lives around.

Raymond Hicks also received numerous awards while working at the Broward Sheriff's Office, including Deputy of the Month in 1997 and for Acts of Bravery in July 1999.

I now understand that when people are accused of wrongdoing, it can make them feel isolated and they may sometimes assume no one understands and no one will fight with them. But Raymond Hicks knew that my family and I were and will always be his prayer worriers, because there is no distance in prayer. I heard Bishop

T.D. Jakes say on television one day that "You face your greatest opposition when you're closest to your biggest miracle." Raymond is aware that this chapter of his life is not about him but it is about what God is going to do in his life. I will continue to support Raymond Hicks in every way.

Raymond has worked diligently and very hard for the last eight years to expose the current sheriff in office. Whether Raymond Hicks chooses to go back to the Sheriff's Office or decides to do something different, God will always smile on him for being faithful. Raymond's mother once said to me, "Coreen, God sits high and he looks low." I now understand what that means. Many people took advantage of the opportunity to use Raymond Hicks' name in the community to get ahead and at the end of the journey they turned their backs on him.

As of this date, many of the same individuals who were directly involved in Raymond Hicks' case are still employed with the Broward Sheriff's Office. The cancer continues within the agency, but Raymond is aware that in the end he will win because what God has blessed no man can curse. I am convinced that Raymond Hicks is aware that he cannot embrace God's forgiveness if he holds on to past wounds. Therefore, he has governed his life in such a way that in order to move into the blessings he must relinquish the pains of the past.

--Coreen Anderson

# APPENDIX

BROWARD COUNTY SHER: 'S OFFICE
STRATEGIC INVESTIGATIONS DIVISION
ARREST/INCIDENT REPORT

| Date: June 15, 2000 | BCN File Number: 10-3779 | | BSO Case Number: N/A | |
|---|---|---|---|---|
| Location of Incident: Various locations throughout Broward | | | | |
| Number of Arrests: 6 | Pending Arrests: 0 | Date of Arrest: 6/15/2000 | | Search Warrant: No |
| Name: Barry Smith | | DOB: 7/21/1967 | Race: Black | Sex: Male |
| Address: 125 NW 6 Avenue, Dania Beach | | | | |
| Charges: Conspriacy to Possess with Intent to Distribute Cocaine/Conspriacy to Commit Money Laundering | | | | |

| Name: Bernard Smith | | DOB: 7/21/1967 | Race: Black | Sex: Male |
|---|---|---|---|---|
| Address: 1525 NW 13 Street, Fort Lauderdale | | | | |
| Charges: Conspriacy to Possess with Intent to Distribute Cocaine / Conspriacy to Commit Money Laundering | | | | |

| Name: Raymond Hicks | | DOB: 6/28/1965 | Race: Black | Sex: Male |
|---|---|---|---|---|
| Address: 3131 NW 43 Place, Fort Lauderdale | | | | |
| Charges: Conspriacy to Possess with Intent to Distribute Cocaine / Conspriacy to Commit Money Laundering | | | | |

| Initiated By: Major Narcotics, South / FBI | | Arrested By: Pisanti / FBI | |
|---|---|---|---|
| Contraband Seized: | | Quantity: | |
| | Federal: ☐   State: ☐ | | |
| Contraband Seized: | | Quantity: | |
| | Federal: ☐   State: ☐ | | |
| Currency Seized: | | Quantity: | |
| | Federal: ☐   State: ☐ | | |
| Vehicle Seized: | | | |
| Firearm Seized: | | | |
| A.O.A. No | Other Agencies Present: FBI, Fort Lauderdale PD, Hollywood PD | | |

Details of Incident:

On 06/15/00 sealed federal indictments were handed down on the six listed suspects in reference to OCDETF case Operation 'Home Team'. The indictments are the culmination of a 3-year investigation run by the Smith brothers in Fort Lauderdale. All the suspects were arrested without incident. Suspect Hicks is a Detention Deputy at the main jail and was suspended by Professional Compliance at the time of his arrest. Suspect Nelson is currently in custody at the Broward County Jail on unrelated charges. No further information at this time.

Page 1 of 2

| Prepared By: Det. R. Pisanti | CCN: 5496 | Approved: Sgt. J. Damiano #2040   Date: 06/16/00 |
|---|---|---|
| For RP | | |

Revised 09/01/99
Form 2

A.2

Uoof

Document #1 (see Ch. 1, p. 2 )

App-1

# Raymond Hicks

## "MISSING" DOCUMENTS TURN UP IN DEPUTY'S LAWSUIT
ELJIN JONES - JULY 25, 2008

http://www.sfltimes.com/uncategorized/missing-documents-turn-up-in-deputys-lawsuit

The Broward Sheriff's Office is not providing any explanations, but a tape recording of a wiretapped phone conversation and other documents that are being described as key evidence in a lawsuit filed against the agency have now surfaced after more than eight years.

Raymond Hicks, 43, of Lauderdale Lakes, filed the lawsuit on April 22, 2004 alleging he was wrongfully fired and maliciously prosecuted on trumped up drug trafficking charges at the hands of BSO brass after complaining about corruption within the department. "After all of this time, we finally have the tape," said Hicks, a former BSO detention deputy who was acquitted of all charges in the drug case. "This tape will help me clear my name," he said.

Hicks said he had not been able to obtain the documents despite making countless public records requests over the past eight years, or so. "They told me they couldn't find it, then they said it was in the court file," he recalled.

"We make it a practice not to discuss pending litigation. This case will be settled through the judicial system, not the media," explained Veda Coleman-Wright, BSO's senior public information officer in an email.

Hicks' attorney, Bruce H. Little, of Fort Lauderdale, had issued subpoenas to get copies of the records, and filed numerous pleadings seeking to have the court to issue an order that would force BSO to hand them over.

In response to an April 2006 motion to compel, BSO submitted a sworn affidavit from internal affairs investigator and Commander Joseph Fitzpatrick.

"The Broward Sheriff's Office, through the Internal Affairs Division as well as through the Records Division and Risk Management, has searched for the tape recording which is the subject of Plaintiff's April 5, 2006 Motion to Compel (and subsequent orders)," wrote Fitzpatrick in an affidavit filed with the court on Feb. 22, 2007.

"The Broward Sheriff's Office has not located the tape and is not presently in possession, custody, or control of the tape," the affidavit further affirmed.

The tape is a recording of a July 23, 1999 wiretapped conversation that took place between Bernard Smith, one of five co-defendants along with Hicks, in the federal drug trafficking case, and then BSO deputy Bernard Brown, III, who is now a detective in the department.

Little did not return calls to the newspaper, but Hicks said, "I believe they intentionally withheld the tape and the other records."

Hicks had been accused of providing confidential department information to the co- defendants. During the trial it was learned it was actually Brown – not Hicks – that is heard during the wiretapped conversation.

Providing confidential investigative information to outsiders violates department policy and doing so could run afoul of state laws.

The tape in question details how Smith, who was under investigation for drug trafficking at the time, made a call to Brown seeking information.

On it, Brown can be heard in a profanity laced phone conversation replete with racial slurs, agreeing to assist Smith in determining what BSO investigators were after when they came looking for one of Smith's brothers.

Brown asked Smith for descriptions of the deputies and suggested they may have been from the fugitive squad, indicating it may have been a possible child support matter.

"...Was it that real big cracker," Brown questioned.

After explaining that the uniforms they wore may not identify the unit they were from, he agreed to check into it.

## Document #2 (see Ch. 3, p. 22)

# I'M STILL STANDING

"But, I can what I'll do tonight is a, while I'm at work I can have one of my girls run his name," the voice, confirmed to be that of Brown's, responded.

Brown went on to ask Smith for his brother's name and date of birth, which Smith said he wasn't sure, but agreed to call Brown right back with that information.

At trial, and while undergoing questioning by federal prosecutor Kathleen Rice, Smith testified that several BSO employees had in fact done favors for him, but he had only asked Brown to run checks on the driver's licenses of family members, nothing more.

Smith denied that Hicks had done any favors for him.

"I don't get personal favors from Raymond Hicks. All me and Raymond Hicks ever do was to spot each other for weights," Smith testified.

During further questioning from Rice, Smith was asked to identify the law enforcement officials who did favors for him.

"Bernard Brown. But I don't call no Raymond Hicks for asking no favors like that," he testified.

Brown could not be reached for comment and did not respond to interview requests sent to him through BSO's Media Relations Department. Smith also named several other BSO deputies. His discussion with Brown, however, is the only one that is supported with a recorded phone conversation.

Following the trial, Fitzpatrick conducted an Internal Affairs investigation into Smith's allegations against Brown. During questioning by Fitzpatrick, Brown acknowledged it was he who is heard on the wiretapped phone conversation agreeing to get the information for Smith.

"That was in the middle of the day, and I was asleep, and um, I think at the time I was working at night, you know on midnight shift at that time, and I don't remember contacting anybody about that information," Brown told Fitzpatrick."I don't remember even getting back to him about any information about that." Brown went on to explain that he and Smith grew up in the same central Broward neighborhood, and that their parents were from the same town in Georgia.

## BROWN PROMOTED

Despite the tape recording detailing the conversation and the testimony from the trial, Brown was cleared of any wrongdoing, as described in a May 17, 2002 final report where the allegations were determined to be unfounded. Brown remains with the department and has been promoted to detective.

After finally being able to review the files, and listen to the recording, Hicks says he has little confidence in the investigation, because it wasn't handled by an outside agency.

"I spent time in jail because they thought it was me on that tape," he said. "My life is destroyed because of this, and after eight long years the tape now appears out of nowhere."

Exactly how, and why the documents have now turned up remains a mystery. BSO has declined to discuss the issue.

Fitzpatrick, who conducted the investigation and submitted the affidavit to the court, did not return calls seeking comment.

Hicks has a theory of what may have taken place and said an independent investigation is warranted.

"I went to BSO, paid a deposit [several weeks ago] and the next day they called to say everything was ready. There are new people in that office, so they just gave it to me," Hicks offered. "I think they handed them over without knowing others in that department had been claiming for years that they did not have them for the past eight years."

He added, "I believe they had the tape all the time, but refused to turn it over because they knew it would show they had no evidence against me."

## Document #2, cont.

# Raymond Hicks

JAILED FOR OVER A YEAR

Once a highly decorated Broward Sheriff's Office corrections deputy for 14 years, Hicks, was arrested on June 15, 2000, along with five other men after BSO and federal agents wrapped up a four-year drug investigation.

After a judge declared he was a possible flight risk, he spent the next 15 months in a Miami federal prison while awaiting trial, which began on Aug. 21, 2001.

By the time defense attorneys and prosecutors had begun their closing arguments more than 30-days later, nearly two-dozen witnesses had been heard.

A 12-person jury on Sept. 26, 2001, took less than 30 minutes to return not-guilty verdicts on all charges, against all of the defendants.

After the verdict was read, U.S. District Court Judge Norman C. Roettger signed an order for all of the defendants to be immediately set free.

Hicks says his entire ordeal began in the early 1990's after he began turning in fellow deputies, whom he had accused of planting evidence on innocent people, and stealing money confiscated from drug suspects during stings.

He has been trying to clear his name ever since and has made several unsuccessful attempts to have the drug case expunged from federal court records.

Hicks said that life has been hard and his family was burdened unnecessarily since his arrest. He has been turned down for numerous jobs, had vehicles repossessed, and the family nearly lost their home to foreclosure.

His eldest daughter was not able to attend college and the family blames it all on the false allegations levied against him.

His lawsuit seeks back pay, loss wages, and unspecified damages for the emotional turmoil he and his family have endured.

He said the newly obtained documents may help in that effort, and in his civil case.

"It's a long, tough fight, but this is a major development, and a blessing from God, so me and my family will just keep on praying," Hicks said.

*EJones@SFLTimes.com*

Document #2, cont.

AO 245A (Rev. 7/87) Judgment of Acquittal

## UNITED STATES DISTRICT COURT

SOUTHERN     DISTRICT OF     FLORIDA

UNITED STATES OF AMERICA

**JUDGMENT OF ACQUITTAL**

V.
RAYMOND HICKS

CASE NUMBER: 00-6162-CR-ROETTGER

The Defendant was found not guilty. IT IS ORDERED that the Defendant is acquitted, discharged, and any bond exonerated.

Signature of Judicial Officer

NORMAN C. ROETTGER
Name and Title of Judicial Officer

26 Sep 2001
Date

Certified to be a true and
correct copy of the document on file
Clarence Maddox, Clerk,
U.S. District Court
Southern District of Florida
By
APR 25 2006
Deputy Clerk
Date

Document #3 (see Ch. 4, p. 28)

# Raymond Hicks

Continuation of FD-302 of ____SOURCE_____, On __11/12/98__ , Page ___2___

accident scene. BARRY SMITH advised that he would handle the
incident. BARRY SMITH allegedly hired a high priced attorney to
handle NELSON's case.

During the week of November 8, 1998, two (2) Unknown
Black Males (UBM) from Fort Myers, Florida, arrived at the
warehouses located at 550 Northwest 27th Avenue, driving a white
Chevrolet Impala. The UBM's came to pick up a package from BARRY
SMITH and return to Fort Myers.

On November 11, 1998, an UBM from Live Oak, Florida,
arrived at the warehouses located at 550 Northwest 27th Avenue,
(Bay B-4). The UBM came to pick up thirty (30) pounds of
marijuana from BARRY SMITH. While the UBM was at the warehouse,
BARRY SMITH advised SAMUEL JONES to activate the scanner, so they
could overhear the UBM cellular telephone conversation to an
unknown party. JONES advised BARRY SMITH that the UBM was okay.

The above incident revealed that BARRY SMITH has a
scanner which is wired in his back office. There is also a
camera in the warehouse which records members of the SMITH
organization having sex.

On November 4, 1998, RAYMOND HICKS was at the
warehouses located at 550 Northwest 27th Avenue, (Bay B-4), for
most of the day. BARRY SMITH gave HICKS a brown paper bag which
contained one-half kilo of cocaine. The Source observed the bag
earlier in the day when BARRY SMITH left it on the water cooler,
and stated, "Don't let it fall in the water."

BARRY SMITH recently purchased a 1999 Lincoln Navigator
(black), bearing Florida license plate GW4 281. The vehicle is
registered to ALEX RAINEY, black male, Date of Birth: August 24,
1959, who is one of BARRY SMITH's truck drivers. The Navigator
is believed not to be a lease and is fully paid for.

Document #4 (see Ch. 4, p. 29)

App-6

**ROADRUCK INVESTIGATIONS, INC.**
4100 N.E. 2nd Avenue
Suite 308
Miami, Florida 33137

STEVEN D. ROADRUCK
PRESIDENT

Offices Located in
Miami
Orlando

RECEIVED
DEC - 7 2000
HUMAN RESOURCES

TELEPHONE
(305) 576-5877
TOLL FREE
1-(877)-498-3154
FAX
(305) 576-5878

November 1, 2000

Broward County Sheriff
Attn: Bea Swirsky/Human Resources
2601 W. Broward Boulevard
Fort Lauderdale, Florida 33310

Dear Ms. Swirsky:

We are respectfully requesting a complete copy of our client's personnel file.

He is an ex Broward Sheriff's Office Corrections Officer (1986-1997).

Raymond Hicks
Black male
DOB 6-28-65
Employee #04693

In addition to the file copies, we need documentation showing that Mr. Hicks was at work on the date, November 4, 1998, please include the time as he states he was working from 6:45 a.m. to 3:00 p.m. and from 3:15 p.m. to 5:30 p.m.

Please contact our office when ready so that we can make arrangements to pick up the copies.

cc. Michelle Russell

Document #5 (see Ch. 6, p.41)

# Raymond Hicks

* (Rev. 10-6-95)

270F-MM-89415, 245F-MM-88061, 245F-MM-

ation of FD-302 of ___SOURCE_____, On _11/12/98_____ . Page __2__

accident scene. BARRY SMITH advised that he would handle the incident. BARRY SMITH allegedly hired a high priced attorney to handle NELSON's case.

During the week of November 8, 1998, two (2) Unknown Black Males (UBM) from Fort Myers, Florida, arrived at the warehouses located at 550 Northwest 27th Avenue, driving a white Chevrolet Impala. The UBM's came to pick up a package from BARRY SMITH and return to Fort Myers.

On November 11, 1998, an UBM from Live Oak, Florida, arrived at the warehouses located at 550 Northwest 27th Avenue, (Bay B-4). The UBM came to pick up thirty (30) pounds of marijuana from BARRY SMITH. While the UBM was at the warehouse, BARRY SMITH advised SAMUEL JONES to activate the scanner, so they could overhear the UBM cellular telephone conversation to an unknown party. JONES advised BARRY SMITH that the UBM was okay.

The above incident revealed that BARRY SMITH has a scanner which is wired in his back office. There is also a camera in the warehouse which records members of the SMITH organization having sex.

On November 4, 1998, RAYMOND HICKS was at the warehouses located at 550 Northwest 27th Avenue, (Bay B-4), for most of the day. BARRY SMITH gave HICKS a brown paper bag which contained one-half kilo of cocaine. The Source observed the bag earlier in the day when BARRY SMITH left it on the water cooler, and stated, "Don't let it fall in the water."

BARRY SMITH recently purchased a 1999 Lincoln Navigator (black), bearing Florida license plate GW4 28I. The vehicle is registered to ALEX RAINEY, black male, Date of Birth: August 24, 1959, who is one of BARRY SMITH's truck drivers. The Navigator is believed not to be a lease and is fully paid for.

Document #6 (see Ch. 6, p.41)

App-8

# I'M STILL STANDING

Shift 2 = ( 7:45Am to 3:00pm

Daily Assignments for Unit: 01 Shift:2   DATE:11/04/98 Wednesday

| st | Title | Lv | Employee | CCN | Status | Time | Total |
|----|-------|----|----------|-----|--------|------|-------|
| 55 | 7TH FLR CTRL B | 21 | CARTER,WILLIAM L | 08699 | | 0800 | 0800 |
| 60 | 7TH FLR HSNG C | 21 | CAMERON,EDDIE J | 06788 | | 0800 | 0800 |
| | | | CAMERON,EDDIE J | 06788 | A00002 | 0800 | 0000 |
| | | | BRAN,RENE | 08471 | 008471 | 0800 | 0800 |
| 65 | 7TH FLR CTRL C | 21 | GOTTFRIED,EDWARD J | 05745 | | 0800 | 0800 |
| 170 | 7TH FLR HSNG D | 21 | JOHNSON,NANCY M | 06768 | | 0800 | 0800 |
| | | | JOHNSON,NANCY M | 06768 | A00003 | 0800 | 0000 |
| | | | MARTIN,HORACE L | 03648 | 003648 | 0800 | 0800 |
| 175 | 7TH FLR CTRL D | 21 | VENTURA,LUIS M | 08532 | | 0800 | 0800 |
| 180 | 7TH FL MVT/UTL | 21 | BLANKS,ANDREA L | 07775 | | 0800 | 0800 |
| 185 | 7TH FL MVT/UTL | 21 | LARSEN,GARRY B | 05078 | | 0800 | 0800 |
| 190 | 7TH FL MVT/UTL | 21 | MARSHALL,DEXTER D | 05138 | | 0800 | 0800 |
| 200 | 6TH FLR HSNG A | 21 | MONTGOMERY,FRED A | 05268 | | 0800 | 0800 |
| 205 | 6TH FLR CTRL A | 21 | WATSON,VANCE L | 06857 | | 0800 | 0800 |
| 210 | 6TH FLR HSNG B | 21 | BATTLE,MARVA O | 04695 | | 0800 | 0800 |
| | | | BATTLE,MARVA O | 04695 | A00021 | 0800 | 0000 |
| | | | MERCADO,HERMAN | 08123 | R02033 | 0800 | 0800 |
| 215 | 6TH FLR CTRL B | 21 | APPLIN,ERIC K | 05702 | | 0800 | 0800 |
| | | | APPLIN,ERIC K | 05702 | A00002 | 0800 | 0000 |
| | | | BUTLER,ANDREA B | 06310 | R02045 | 0800 | 0800 |
| 220 | 6TH FLR HSNG C | 21 | BELLINGER,GEORGE | 06023 | | 0800 | 0800 |
| 225 | 6TH FLR CTRL C | 21 | CONNORS,DANIEL W | 07522 | | 0800 | 0800 |
| 230 | 6TH FLR HSNG D | 21 | JACKSON,JOEY L | 07800 | | 0800 | 0800 |
| 235 | 6TH FLR CTRL D | 21 | HICKS,RAYMOND L | 04693 | | 0800 | 0800 |
| 240 | 6TH FL MVT/UTL | 21 | SMALL,SCOTT M | 07802 | | 0800 | 0800 |
| 245 | 6TH FL MVT/UTL | 21 | WARD,ELSA L | 04836 | | 0800 | 0800 |
| 250 | 6TH FL MVT/UTL | 21 | DELIFUS,GEORGE E | 04937 | | 0800 | 0800 |
| 260 | 5TH FLR HSNG A | 21 | KIMBROUGH,VINCENT L | 05692 | | 0800 | 0800 |
| | | | KIMBROUGH,VINCENT L | 05692 | A00002 | 0800 | 0000 |
| | | | WALDEN,MONICA L | 06452 | R02031 | 0800 | 0800 |
| 265 | 5TH FLR CTRL A | 21 | WILLIAMS,DARRELL O | 05307 | | 0800 | 0800 |
| 270 | 5TH FLR HSNG B | 21 | PHILLIPS,MICHAEL S | 05726 | | 0800 | 0800 |
| | | | PHILLIPS,MICHAEL S | 05726 | A00021 | 0800 | 0000 |
| | | | BERRY,TIFFANNIE | 08866 | 008866 | 0800 | 0800 |
| 275 | 5TH FLR CTRL B | 21 | BOSLEY,CHARLES J | 06338 | | 0800 | 0800 |
| | | | BOSLEY,CHARLES J | 06338 | A00002 | 0800 | 0000 |
| | | | MOLIN,KATHI M | 08631 | E08631 | 0800 | 0800 |
| 280 | 5TH FLR HSNG C | 21 | CARTER,MAURICE | 06685 | | 0800 | 0800 |
| 285 | 5TH FLR CTRL C | 21 | MOULTRY,LOUIS L | 04703 | | 0800 | 0800 |
| | | | MOULTRY,LOUIS L | 04703 | A00021 | 0800 | 0000 |
| | | | SMITH,STEPHANIE D | 08110 | R02040 | 0800 | 0800 |
| 290 | 5TH FLR HSNG D | 21 | SMITH,JAMIE D | 08363 | | 0800 | 0800 |
| 295 | 5TH FLR CTRL D | 21 | MCCLOVER,JONATHAN T | 07527 | | 0800 | 0800 |
| | | | MCCLOVER,JONATHAN T | 07527 | A00021 | 0800 | 0000 |
| | | | MIDDLETON,RORY | 05016 | R02034 | 0800 | 0800 |
| 300 | 5TH FL MVT/UTL | 21 | MCKEON,ROBERT W | 05200 | | 0800 | 0800 |
| 305 | 5TH FL MVT/UTL | 21 | BARBARA,JAMES A | 04013 | | 0800 | 0800 |
| 310 | 5TH FL MVT/UTL | 21 | JACKSON,LISA R | 04854 | | 0800 | 0800 |
| 320 | 4TH FLR HSNG A | 21 | STEWART,ALVIN D | 05913 | | 0800 | 0800 |
| 325 | 4TH FLR CTRL A | 21 | YOUNG,VERNIDEAN T | 05517 | | 0800 | 0800 |
| 330 | 4TH FLR HSNG B | 21 | LONG,JIMMIE C | 07924 | | 0800 | 0800 |

Document #7 (see Ch. 6, p.41)

App-9

Document #8 (see Ch. 5, p. 38)

**Deputy of The Month**

★ ★ ★ ★ ★

In recognition of outstanding performance

*Deputy Raymond Hicks*

is hereby presented with this certificate of Deputy of the Month for March. In recognition of exceptional work performance and commitment to the goals set forth by the Broward Sheriff's Office.

**1997**

PRESENTED ON APRIL SECOND
NINETEEN HUNDRED NINETY SEVEN

**Deputy of the Month**

In recognition of outstanding performance

*Deputy Raymond Hicks*

is hereby presented with this certificate of Deputy of the Month for July, 1999. In recognition of exceptional work performance and commitment to the goals set forth by the Broward Sheriff's Office.

**1999**

PRESENTED ON AUGUST FIRST,
NINETEEN HUNDRED NINETY NINE

Document #9 (see Ch. 5, p. 39)

# Raymond Hicks

| CIS # | 540001159 | | BCCN # | 0 | | | | | | | ng Sheet Control Date and Time |
|---|---|---|---|---|---|---|---|---|---|---|

| OBTS | 0 | | Print Clearance | | | Prints No | | | 01/11/00 12:32:37 |

| Arrest # | LL 0001159 | | Offense Report # | | | Agency LL |

**Last Name**
First   PRATT , ANCEL ,
Middle

SSN # 264313788

| Race | Sex | Height | Weight | Eyes | Hair | Comp. | Age | DOB | Place of Birth | State | FDLE |
|---|---|---|---|---|---|---|---|---|---|---|---|
| BLACK | M | 508 | 220 | BRN | BLK | DRK | 43 | 12/08/1956 | MIAMI | FL | 0 |

| Permanent Address | 2760 NW 35 AV | | | LAUDERDALE LAKES   FL  33311 | Months of Residence 0 |

| Arrest Date 1/10/00 10:30:00 | Arresting Officer SMITH | Place of Arrest 2760 NW 35 | Badge Number 8202 |

| Inmate Logged Date 1/11/00 12:03:06   Inmate Log Type FULL INTAKE | Place Admitted MAIN |

Intake Comments:29/54 6552 W/C

Alias Last name, First, Middle

Scars,Marks,Tattoos:

| Release Date/Time | | Release Reason | | Release Authorized By |
|---|---|---|---|---|

| Charge No. | Charge Initiation Date | Statute | Case Number | Level | Mag.Code | Type | Bond Amount |
|---|---|---|---|---|---|---|---|
| 1 | 01/11/2000 12:29 | 784.021-1a(C) | | 3F | N | BD | 5000 |

Charges AGG ASSAULT W/FIRE ARM     Comments

| Booking Off. ID bs04097 | County | Judge |

' End of Report '

Document #10 (see Ch. 6, p. 42)

App-12

# I'm Still Standing

**Ilene Lieberman, Mayor**
e-mail: ilieberman@broward.org

March 5, 2004

Desirée H. Barnes, Aide
Sharon Kerbis, Admin. Coordinator
954-357-7001
FAX 954-357-7295

First Sgt. Raymond L. Hicks
C/o JM Family Enterprises, Inc.
111 N.W. 12th Avenue
Deerfield Beach, FL   33443

Dear First Sgt. Hicks:

Please allow me to congratulate you on the well-deserved honor of being one of the recipients of the 2004 African American Achievers Award from JM Family Enterprises. I am very pleased that you have received this recognition for all of your work in the South Florida community.

Again, congratulations on this prestigious award, and thank you for all of your efforts on behalf of the community.

Sincerely,

Ilene Lieberman
Broward County Mayor

ILM/slk

Board of County Commissioners, 115 South Andrews Avenue, Room 414, Fort Lauderdale, Florida 33301-1801

Document #11 (see Ch. 6, p. 46)

# Raymond Hicks

Broward Sheriff's Office
2001 West Broward Boulevard
Fort Lauderdale, Florida 33312
(954) 831-8900 • www.sheriff.org

July 06, 2005

Raymond Hicks
3131 NW 43rd Place
Oakland Park, FL 33309

Re:  Separation Date

Dear Raymond Hicks:

Per our discussion, the Florida Department of Law Enforcement's Automated Management System was updated to reflect your separation date from the Broward Sheriff's Office as October 6, 2003.

Should you have any questions on the above, please feel free to contact this office at (954) 321-4412

Sincerely,

Heather Bryan
Human Resources Coordinator
Human Resources Bureau
Broward Sheriff's Office

/hb

Document #12 (see Ch. 6, p. 46)

App-14

COUNTY COURT DISPOSITION ORDER IN AND FOR BROWARD COUNTY, FLORIDA

DATE: _____ CASE NO. 04000243MM20A _____ ARREST NO. _____ BCCN NO. _____

State of Florida VS HICKS, RAYMOND _____ AKA _____

Cash Bond /Surety _____ Amount $ _____ Estreated _____ Vacated _____ Return to Dep. _____

Cash Bond /Surety _____ Amount $ _____ Estreated _____ Vacated _____ Return to Dep. _____

( ) REMANDED ( ) REMAIN I/C ( ) UNTIL PICKED UP: _____ OR BED AVAILABLE AT _____
( ) Magistrates ( ) First VOP ( ) Guilty ( ) No Information
( ) Arraignments ( ) Final VOP ( ) No Contest ( ) Adj. Guilty
( ) Change of Plea ( ) PSI ( ) Admits / Denies Allegations ( ) Adj. Withheld
( ) Trial by Jury ( ) Sentencing ( ) Convicted by Jury/Court ( ) Nolle Prosequi
( ) Trial by Court ( ) Acquitted by Jury/Court ( ) Dismissed
( ) Adj. and Sentence Deferred to: _____ PSI: YES _____ NO _____

CHARGES:
DISCHARGE FIREARM PUBLIC

SENTENCE:
COUNT(S) _____ Non-Probation Sentence
COUNT(S) _____ Reporting Probation _____ Months with Special Conditions:
( ) DUI School Level _____ ( ) Evaluation, treatment and therapy, if necessary
( ) May work off fine / costs @ $ _____ per hour ( ) May buy out community service @ $ _____ per hour
( ) _____ hours community service ( ) _____ AA meeting(s) per week
( ) _____ days immobilization by:
( ) No alcohol or intoxicants while on probation ( ) Random breath / urine analysis @ defendant's expense
( ) License suspended _____ ( ) DDS _____ hours ( ) Anger Management _____
( ) Pay all outstanding fines / costs on Driver's License Record. ( ) Shoplifters Program
( ) All fines / costs imposed are a condition of probation on Count(s) _____
( ) Time Served _____ days on Count(s) _____
( ) _____ days Broward County Jail with credit for _____ days time served.
( ) No harmful contact / ( ) No contact with victim
( ) All special conditions of probation must be met by the _____ month of probation.
( ) Early termination of probation upon completion of all special conditions.
( ) All non-monetary conditions of probation must be completed by _____
( ) OTHER: STATES MOTION for Continuance DENIED

| COUNT | FINE | CC | 5% | VC | CJC | SN1 | AC | JJ | CSTF | CFF | OTF | CDC | EMTF | DVC | TOTA |
|-------|------|----|----|----|----|----|----|----|----|----|----|----|----|----|----|
| | | | | | | | | | | | | | | | |
| | | | | | | | | | | | | | | | |
| | | | | | | | | | | | | | | | |
| | | | | | | | | | | | | | | | |

PAYMENT BY CREDIT CARD: CALL (954) 712-7___. MAIL PAYMENT TO CLERK OF CO
P.O. BOX 94610, FT LAUDERDALE, FL 33302-4610. YOU MUST PAY YOUR FINES AND/
OR COSTS BY _____, 20__. IF YOU FAIL TO PAY, YOU MUST ATTEND A FAILURE-TO
PAY-FINE HEARING ON _____, 20__ $ _____ ROOM _____ AT THE
NORTH SATELLITE COURTHOUSE, 1600 WEST HILLSBORO BLVD, DEERFIELD BE
_____. FAILURE TO ATTEND THIS HEARING SHALL RESULT IN A WARRANT FOR YOU
ARREST. LATE FEES MAY BE ADDED, AND/OR YOUR LICENSE MAY BE SUSPENDED.

JUDGE _____ DEPUTY CLERK _____
DEFENDANT

Document #13 (see Ch. 6, p. 47)

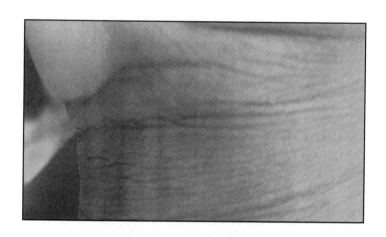

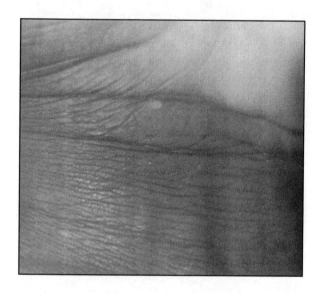

Document #14 (see Ch. 6, p. 47)

1 of 1

CIRCUIT COURT DISPOSITION ORDER IN AND FOR BROWARD COUNTY, FLORIDA
Case Number __05012432CF10A__  Arrest Number _____ BCCN # _____
State of Florida VS __HICKS, RAYMOND__ _____ AKA _____
Judge __MARC H GOLD__ _____ Cash bond / Return to depositor / Surety bond / IC
Cash bond number(s) _____
Charges: __002 CHILD ABUSE__

( ) REMANDED ( ) REMAIN IC ( ) UNTIL PICKED UP BY _____ OR
BED AVAILABLE AT

( ) Arraignment  ( ) Change of Plea  ( ) Guilty  ( ) No Contest  ( ) PSI/PDR  ( ) Sentencing / Re-Sentencing
( ) Trial by Jury  ( ) Trial by Court  ( ) First VOP / VOCC  ( ) Final VOP / VOCC  ( ) Admits Allegations
( ) Convicted by Jury/Court _____  ( ) Acquitted by Jury /Court _____  ( ) Dismissed _____  ( ) Speedy
( ) Discharged _____  (X) Nolle Prosequi _____  ( ) Found Incompetent/Committed to Child/Family Services
( ) Adj. Guilty _____  ( ) Adj. Withheld _____  ( ) Adj. Delinquent _____
( ) Committed to DJJ/Level _____  ( ) Sentence Withheld  ( ) Previous Sentence Vacated
( ) PSI Ordered _____
Adj. and Sentence deferred to _____

Type of Probation / Community Control:
( ) Youthful Offender  ( ) Drug Offender  ( ) Sexual Offender  ( ) Habitual Offender  ( ) Mental Health  ( ) County
PROBATION/COMM. CONTROL:  ( ) Revoked  ( ) Reinstated  ( ) Modified  ( ) Terminated
( ) Extended _____  ( ) All previous special conditions apply
WARRANT:  ( ) Dismissed  ( ) Withdrawn  ( ) Served in open court

SENTENCE: (PROBATION/COMM.CONTROL)
COUNT(S): _____
_____ ( ) Years  ( ) Months  ( ) Days  ( ) Probation  ( ) Community Control  ( ) followed by
_____ ( ) Years  ( ) Months  ( ) Days  ( ) Probation  ( ) Community Control
( ) each count concurrent/consecutive  ( ) concurrent  ( ) consecutive to case number _____
COUNT(S): _____
_____ ( ) Years  ( ) Months  ( ) Days  ( ) Probation  ( ) Community Control  ( ) followed by
_____ ( ) Years  ( ) Months  ( ) Days  ( ) Probation  ( ) Community Control
( ) each count concurrent/consecutive  ( ) concurrent  ( ) consecutive to case number _____

SENTENCE: (INCARCERATION)
COUNT(S): _____  ( ) One year plus one day ( ) _____ ( ) Years ( ) Months ( ) Days
( ) BCJ  ( ) FSP, w/credit for _____ days T/S
( ) followed by _____ ( ) Years  ( ) Months  ( ) Days  ( ) Probation  ( ) Community Control
( ) each count concurrent/consecutive  ( ) concurrent/consecutive ( ) to case number _____
( ) any other sentence  ( ) Work release  ( ) prison sentence suspended
COUNT(S): _____  ( ) One year plus one day ( ) _____ ( ) Years ( ) Months ( ) Days
( ) BCJ  ( ) FSP, w/credit for _____ days T/S
( ) followed by _____ ( ) Years  ( ) Months  ( ) Days  ( ) Probation  ( ) Community Control
( ) each count concurrent/consecutive  ( ) concurrent/consecutive ( ) to case number _____
( ) any other sentence  ( ) Work release  ( ) prison sentence suspended

JUDGE _____
DEPUTY CLERK _____  DATE __8/14/06__
                          DEFENDANT
98-1  )CC 14-1 REV. 9/01

Document #15 (see Ch. 6, p. 49)

# Raymond Hicks

IN THE CIRCUIT COURT OF THE
17TH JUDICIAL CIRCUIT, IN AND FOR
BROWARD COUNTY, FLORIDA

CASE NO: 04-6719 CACE 11

RAYMOND HICKS,

JUDGE: BARRY E. GOLDSTEIN

    Plaintiff,

vs.

BROWARD SHERIFF'S OFFICE,

    Defendant.

_____/

## PLAINTIFF'S SWORN MOTION TO DISQUALIFY

COMES NOW, the Plaintiff, RAYMOND HICKS, by and through his undersigned counsel pursuant to Rule 2.330 Florida Judicial Administration Rule and Florida Statute 38.10 (2007), and herein moves to disqualify the Trial Judge in this case, Barry E. Goldstein, and as grounds therefore would show:

1. In preparation for trial on this case the undersigned was advised by a fellow attorney on April 4, 2008 that the possibility existed that the trial judge, Judge Barry E. Goldstein, has a brother who has a high ranking official in the Broward County Sheriff's Office. The undersigned has no prior knowledge of this, nor had it been disclosed by the Court or opposing counsel.

2. This case involves substantial issues with regard to credibility of certain members of BSO as well as legal issues raised with the Court on the liability of members of the Broward County Sheriff's Office with regard to the issues raised by the Plaintiff.

3. Immediately upon learning this information, the undersigned undertook an investigation to determine whether in fact the information was correct and although it could not be

Document #16 (see Ch. 7, pp. 53-54)

actually verified, it was determined that there was individual by the name of Michael Goldstein who is a Major with the Broward County Sheriff's Office who's rumored to be related to Judge Barry E. Goldstein. That person has held positions in Road Patrol and Human Resources during the time period covered by the facts in this case.

4.   By his signature affixed hereto, Raymond Hicks fears that he will not receive a fair trial or hearing because of a potential prejudice or bias of the Judge as the Judge is related to an individual who has close ties with the Broward County Sheriff's Office and may be in the chain of command of the individuals who will testify in this case and whose credibility will be questioned.

5.   After beginning the investigation on this matter, the undersigned contacted counsel for the Broward County Sheriff's Office who verified that Michael Goldstein was a Major until the recent past with the Broward County Sheriff's Office, and he in fact is the brother of Barry E. Goldstein, the Judge.

**WHEREFORE**, the undersigned herein moves this court for an Order of Recuse of Barry E. Goldstein as the presiding Judge in the above styled case.

## ATTESTATION BY RAYMOND HICKS, PLAINTIFF

I, Raymond Hicks, do hereby swear and affirm that I have read this motion and attest that it is my belief that I do not believe that I will receive a fair trial in this matter based upon my belief that the presiding Judge, Barry E. Goldstein, will be biased in favor of the Broward County Sheriff's Office and it's members.

RAYMOND HICKS

STATE OF FLORIDA    )
COUNTY OF BROWARD )

BEFORE ME, the undersigned authority, an officer duly authorized to take

Document #16, cont.

App-19

# Raymond Hicks

acknowledgments and administer oaths, the foregoing instrument was acknowledged before me this 4th day of April, 2008, by **RAYMOND HICKS**, who is personally known to me, who after being first duly sworn according to law, deposes and says that he has read and executed the foregoing instrument and that the facts contained therein are true and correct to the best of his knowledge and belief.

DATED at Fort Lauderdale, Florida, this 4th day of April, 2008.

My Commission Expires:

BRUCE H. LITTLE
MY COMMISSION # DO 375503
EXPIRES: March 28, 2009
Bonded Thru Notary Public Underwriters

BRUCE H. LITTLE

Notary Public

## CERTIFICATE OF SERVICE

**I HEREBY CERTIFY** that a true and correct copy of the foregoing was furnished via facsimile to 954-463-2444 and First Class U.S. Mail to Mike Piper, Esq., 2455 E. Sunrise Blvd., Suite 1000, Fort Lauderdale, FL, 33304; and via facsimile to 954-764-5367 and U.S. Mail to Robert C. Meacham, Esq., One Financial Plaza, Suite 2602, Fort Lauderdale, FL 33394 on this 4th day of April, 2008.

BRUCE H. LITTLE, P.A.
Attorney for Plaintiff
645 SE 5th Terrace
Fort Lauderdale, Florida 33301-3160
Phone No.: 954-523-3299
Fax No.: 954-765-0545

By: _____
BRUCE H. LITTLE, ESQ.
F.B.No.: 284580

Document #16, cont.

App-20

IN THE CIRCUIT COURT OF THE 17<sup>TH</sup>
JUDICIAL CIRCUIT, IN AND FOR
BROWARD COUNTY, FLORIDA

CASE NO.: 04-6719-11

RAYMOND HICKS,

Plaintiff,

vs.

KENNETH C. JENNE, as Sheriff
of Broward County,

Defendant.

_____/

## A F F I D A V I T

STATE OF FLORIDA

COUNTY OF BROWARD

BEFORE ME, the undersigned authority, personally appeared Joseph Fitzpatrick, who, being by me first duly sworn, on oath, deposes and says as follows:

1. My name is Joseph Fitzpatrick and I am employed as a sworn law enforcement officer with the Broward Sheriff's Office.

2. I presently am the Commander of the Internal Affairs Division at the Broward Sheriff's Office.

3. I have personal knowledge of the facts contained herein.

4. The Broward Sheriff's Office, through the Internal Affairs Division as well as through the Records Division and Risk Management Division , has searched

EXHIBIT

"17"

Document #17 (see Ch. 7, p. 55)

App-21

for the tape recording which is the subject of Plaintiff's April 5, 2006 Motion to Compel (and subsequent orders). The Broward Sheriff's Office has not located the tape and is not presently in possession, custody, or control of the tape.

5.     The Broward Sheriff's Office previously has produced to Plaintiff all relevant tape recordings in its possession, custody, and control.

FURTHER AFFIANT SAITH NAUGHT.

_____
Joseph Fitzpatrick

STATE OF FLORIDA

COUNTY OF BROWARD

BEFORE ME, the undersigned authority, personally appeared Joseph Fitzpatrick , who, after first showing the proper identification of _____, or being personally known to me, was duly sworn, deposes and says that he/she has read the foregoing and that the same is true and correct to the best of his/her knowledge and belief.

SWORN TO AND SUBSCRIBED to before me this 22 day of February , 2007.

_____
Notary Public

My Commission Expires:

Document #17, cont.

IN THE CIRCUIT COURT OF THE
17TH JUDICIAL CIRCUIT, IN AND FOR
BROWARD COUNTY, FLORIDA

RAYMOND HICKS,

CASE NO: 04-6719 CACE 18

Plaintiff,

vs.

AL LAMBERTI, as Sheriff of
Broward County,

Defendant.

_____/

## PLAINTIFF'S MOTION FOR RELIEF FROM JUDGMENT AND INCORPORATED MEMORANDUM OF LAW

**COMES NOW** the Plaintiff, RAYMOND HICKS, by and through his undersigned counsel pursuant to Florida Rules of Civil Procedure 1.540(b)(4), and herein moves this Court for Relief From Judgment rendered by this Court and as grounds therefore would show:

1.    This case was before the Court on its trial calendar and while awaiting trial the parties were advised that the court was referring it to a retired judge, by the name of Eli Breger, who would preside over the trial.

2.    This action in appointing a retired judge to hear the case would appear to have been accomplished pursuant to Administrative Order I-92-J-1 of the 17th Judicial Circuit, in and for Broward County, Florida (copy attached as Exhibit "1".)

3.    The beginning of trial, both counsel inquired of Judge Breger as to his legal authority to hear the case, based upon the fact that he was a retired County Court judge from Dade County, Florida.

4.    Judge Breger advised the parties' counsel that there was a Supreme Court Order

ϡ

Document #18 (see Ch. 7, p. 58)

App-23

# Raymond Hicks

allowing him to hear the case as a retired county court judge. The trial commenced and ultimately resulted in a Final Judgment rendered by the Court on May 23, 2009, (copy attached as Exhibit "2".)

5.      Counsel for the Plaintiff attempted to find the Order allowing Judge Breger to hear the case and ultimately determined that no order was ever done.

6.      On or about May 28, 2009, the undersigned received an email from the General Counsel of the 17th Judicial Circuit, (copy attached as Exhibit "3"), attaching an Administrative Order allegedly rendered by the court on May 28, 2009 "nunc pro tunc" to May 11, 2009. The essence of the Order allegedly appointed Eli Breger as Senior Judge for temporary duty to the Circuit Court in and for the 17th Judicial Circuit to hear the case of Raymond Hicks vs. BSO, et al.

7.      It is the Plaintiff's position herein that the Order rendered by the Court on May 28, 2009, nunc pro tunc to May 11, 2009, ineffectively attempted to vest Judge Breger with jurisdiction retroactively and as such the Final Judgment rendered by Judge Breger is void.

## MEMORANDUM OF LAW

The appointment of senior and retirement judges has been reviewed within Florida juris prudence for a number of years. In 2003, the Florida Supreme Court adopted a Report and Recommendations of the Committee on the Appointment and Assignment of Senior Judges, 847 So.2d 415 (Fla. 2003), determining that the availability of senior judges and improves the service of Florida courts. This has been an issue for a number of years. Likewise, the Court has

2

Document #18, cont.

App-24

# I'm Still Standing

addressed the issue of retired judges and their appointment to active service, and formulated rules governing the assignment to duty of retirement judges, justices, and judges, 239 So.2d 254 (Fla.1970). The issue has also not been without litigation. The Florida Supreme Court in 1985 heard the case of Crusoe v. Rowls, 472 So.2d 1163 (Fla. 1985), wherein the issue involved the proper extent, duration, and purposes of assigning county court judge to perform circuit court jurisdiction work. The court resolved the subject determining that a county court judge can be assigned to circuit court for a "relatively short time". But that the "assignment cannot usurp, supplant, or effectively deprive circuit court jurisdiction of a particular type of case on a permanent basis." In addition, the Florida Supreme Court laid to rest whether a county court judge can be indefinitely assigned a circuit court duty in the case of Payret v. Adams, 500 So.2d 136 (Fla.1986). In addition, in the year 2003, the Florida Supreme Court decided a case out of Broward County, Florida, concerning the appointment of a senior judge. In the case of Physicians Health Care Plans, Inc., v. Pfeifler, 846 So.2d 1129(Fla. 2003), the Florida Supreme Court decided that "temporary duty in any court for which the judge is qualified and to delegate to a chief judge of a judicial circuit the power to assign judges for duty in that circuit." It was the Supreme Court's authority, to do so, pursuant to article V, section 2(a) of the Florida Constitution. In addition, the court opined that Florida Rule of Judicial Administration 2.050(b)(4) delegates the chief justice's assignment power to the chief judges of the judicial circuits to "assign any judge to temporary service for which the judge is qualified in any court in the same circuit."

3

Document #18, cont.

# Raymond Hicks

·

It would, therefore, appear that even though Judge Breger was not elected in Broward County, Florida, as a circuit court judge, he could be appointed based upon his prior services as a county court judge. Without that "appointment," he is without "authority," and not "qualified." The thrust of the Plaintiff's argument herein involves the retrospective granting of jurisdiction of Judge Breger by the "nunc pro tunc Order". The term "nunc pro tunc" is defined by Black's Law Dictionary, 3rd Edition, P.1267, as follows: "a nunc pro tunc entry is an entry made now, as something which was actually previously done, to have effect as to the former date. Its office is not to supply omitted action by the court, but to supply an omission in the record of action really had where entry thereof was omitted through inadvertence or mistake." D.M. v. State, 580 So.2d 634 (Fla. 1st DCA 1991).

It is Plaintiff's argument herein, that the vesting of jurisdiction is a much more formal determination and process, and if Judge Breger had no jurisdiction to enter the Final Judgment in this case then the Final Judgment is void. This can be seen in other situations such as in the case of Carter v. Dorman, 385 So.2d 740 (Fla. 3rd DCA, 1980) where the Court determined that where an original judgment was entered without jurisdiction while an appeal from a non final trial order was pending but that judgement was void. Although it should be pointed out that after making such decision the appellate court determined that the trial court would have jurisdiction to enter a new final judgment, but that is factually distinguishable from what occurred *subjudice*. In addition, Florida courts for a substantial period of time determined that the jurisdictional powers of such offices of magistrate are limited and actions taken by them without jurisdiction are void,

4

Document #18, cont.

App-26

# I'M STILL STANDING

Lackner v. Central Florida Investments, Inc., Case No. 5D07-3542 (Fla. 5th DCA 2009). There have been instances where appellate courts have determined that circuit courts entering orders during the pendency of an appeal failed to have jurisdiction to enter such order even when done nunc pro tunc, Chapman v. Universal Underwriters Ins. Co., 549 So.2d 679 (Fla. 1st DCA 1989).

The entry of the order by the Chief Judge subjudice investing jurisdiction in Judge Breger "nunc pro tunc" constituted a void action. Although nunc pro tunc orders can be done for housekeeping purposes, entry of an order conferring jurisdiction nunc pro tunc is a void action. Fiehe v. R.E. Householder Company, 98 Fla. 627, 125 So.2 (Fla. 1929).

Judge Breger, until entry of the order appointing him to the circuit court, had no jurisdiction to enter any order or final judgment in this case. The "nunc pro tunc" Order should not be used as a vehicle to retroactively vest Judge Breger with jurisdiction and as such the Final Judgment should be determined to be void and Plaintiff should be granted a new trial herein.

**WHEREFORE**, the undersigned herein moves this Court for an order determining that the Final Judgment rendered by Judge Breger is void and resetting this case for trial on the next docket.

## CERTIFICATE OF SERVICE

**I HEREBY CERTIFY** that a true and correct copy of the foregoing was furnished via First Class U.S. Mail to: Michael R. Piper, Esq., Johnson, Anselmo, Murdoch, Burke, Piper & Hochman, P.A., 2455 E. Sunrise Blvd., Suite 1000, Fort Lauderdale, FL, 33304; Nancy Little Hoffman, P.A., 6550 N. Federal Highway, Ste. 511, Fort Lauderdale, FL 33308; and Robert C.

5

Document #18, cont.

App-27

# Raymond Hicks

Meacham, Esq., One Financial Plaza, Suite 2602, Fort Lauderdale, FL 33394 on this 6th day of

July, 2009.

BRUCE H. LITTLE, P.A.
Attorney for Plaintiff
645 SE 5th Terrace
Fort Lauderdale, Florida 33301
Phone No.: 954-523-3299
Fax No.: 954-765-0545

By: _____
BRUCE H. LITTLE, ESQ.
F.B.No.: 284580

STATE OF FLORIDA
BROWARD COUNTY
I DO HEREBY CERTIFY the within and foregoing is a true
and correct copy of the original as it appears on record
and file in the office of the Circuit Court Clerk of Broward
County, Florida.
WITNESS my hand and Official Seal at Fort Lauderdale
Florida, this the _____ day of MAR 18 2015
Clerk of the Court

Deputy Clerk

6

Document #18, cont.

App-28

# I'M STILL STANDING

Subj:     **Hicks v. BSO**
Date:     5/28/2009 4:05:17 P.M. Eastern Daylight Time
From:     arieman@17th.flcourts.org
To:       brucehlittle@aol.com

Mr. Little

At the request of your assistant Mary Ann, attached is an electronic copy of the Administrative
Order signed by Chief Judge Tobin assigning Judge Breger to hear Hicks v. BSO. If you require a
true or certified copy of the Administrative Order, please contact Howard C. Forman, Clerk of
Court, as he is the custodian of all original court records.
Alexandra V. Rieman
General Counsel
17th Judicial Circuit
Broward County Courthouse
201 S.E. Sixth Street
Fort Lauderdale, Florida 33301
954-831-7560

NOTICE: Pursuant to Florida Rule Judicial Administration 2.420 your e-mail address
may be subject to public access upon request for records. If you do not want your
e-mail address released in response to a records request, do not send electronic
mail to this entity. Instead, contact this office by phone or in writing.

Thursday, May 28, 2009 AOL: BRUCEHLITTLE

Exhibit "3"

Document #19 (see Ch. 7, p. 59)

# Raymond Hicks

IN THE CIRCUIT COURT OF THE SEVENTEENTH
JUDICIAL CIRCUIT IN AND FOR BROWARD COUNTY, FLORIDA

Order Number 2009-63-Temp

**ADMINISTRATIVE ORDER
TEMPORARILY APPOINTING SENIOR JUDGE TO CIRCUIT COURT**

In accordance with the authority vested in the chief judge by Florida Rule of Judicial Administration 2.215, it is ordered:

The Honorable Eli Breger, Senior Judge, is assigned to temporary duty in the Circuit Court of the Seventeenth Judicial Circuit, Civil Division for the purpose of hearing and disposing of any and all matters, including but not limited to pretrial, trial, and post trial matters, which may be presented to him for a judicial determination in the following case:

| Case No. | Style |
|----------|-------|
| CACE 04-6719-18 | *Raymond Hicks vs. BSO, et al* |

The Honorable Eli Breger shall have all the power and jurisdiction of a Circuit Judge in the above referenced case.

DONE AND ORDERED in chambers at Fort Lauderdale, Broward County, Florida on May 28, 2009 nunc pro tunc to May 11, 2009.

s/Victor Tobin
Victor Tobin, Chief Judge

Document #20 (see Ch. 7, p. 59)

App-30

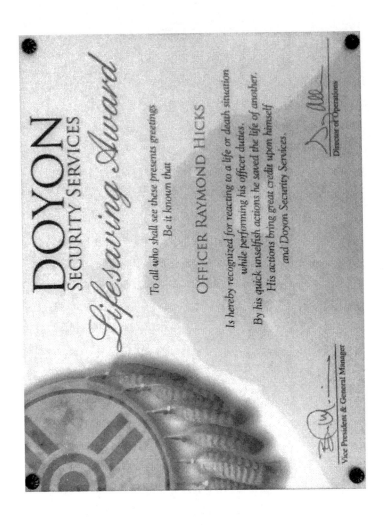

Document #21 (see Ch. 7, p. 63 )

# Raymond Hicks

UNITED STATES DISTRICT COURT
SOUTHERN DISTRICT OF FLORIDA
FT. LAUDERDALE DIVISION

United States of America,

          Plaintiff,

vs

Barry Smith, et al.

          Defendants.

_____/

Case No. 00-6162-CR-ROETTGERS

To whom it may concern:

I, **Barry Smith,** After first being duly sworn, do depose and say:

1.    That I am a co-defendant in the matter of U.S. of America v. Raymond Hicks, et al, case no. 00-6162-CR-Roettgers.

2.    That at the present, I do not know if I will testify at my own trial.

3.    That at a separate trial, if placed under subpoena, I would testify on behalf of my co-defendant **Raymond Hicks** as follows:

> A.  That I never paid Raymond Hicks money for police type favors, or confidential police-type information.
>
> B.  That Raymond Hicks lawfully purchased my Mercedes Benz automobile.
>
> C.  That since I am not guilty of having distributed cocaine, Raymond Hicks could never have transported cocaine for me.
>
> D.  That I do not believe or know that Raymond Hicks was ever involved in any illegal activity including drug activity.

-1-

Document #22 (see Ch. 8, p. 67 )

# I'M STILL STANDING

E. That I have never heard Raymond Hicks
say that he would "badge his way out
of trouble it ever stopped by police"

Sincerely,

**BARRY SMITH**

### NOTARY

The foregoing instrument was acknowledged before me this _23rd_ day of
_April_ 2001, by _Barry Smith_ who had produced Federal Detention
Center-Miami, Florida Inmate card#:_55844-004_ as Identification and who is not
personally known by me.

_Adrienne Lamb_
NOTARY PUBLIC—STATE OF FLORIDA

NOTARY PUBLIC—STATE OF FLORIDA

_–2–_

Document #22, cont.

App-33

# Raymond Hicks

February 25, 2001

To Whom It May Concern:

I, Earl Parker, being of sound mind and body due hereby state that never at any time did I combine, conspire, or agree to possess cocaine with the intent to distribute with Raymond Hicks. In my opinion Raymond Hicks is one of the most respected individuals within community. For many years he has demonstrated great concern for our neighborhood's youth and elderly. I cannot imagine that Mr. Hicks would ever, or has ever been involved in any illegal activity. I pray this statement will assist in freeing Raymond Hicks, who is an innocent man.

Sincerely,

Earl Parker

Earl Parker

The foregoing instrument was acknowledged before me this 26<sup>th</sup> day of February 2001, by Earl Parker who had produced Federal Detention Center Miami, Florida Inmate Card # 53346-004 as indentification, and who is not personally known by me.

Tracie E. Jones
Notary Public-State of Florida

OFFICIAL NOTARY SEAL
TRACIE E JONES
NOTARY PUBLIC STATE OF FLORIDA
COMMISSION NO. CC761233
MY COMMISSION EXP. JULY 20,2002

Tracie E. Jones
Notary Public-Printed Name

DEFENDANT'S
EXHIBIT

4

Document #22, cont.

App-34

# I'M STILL STANDING

March 13, 2001

### TO WHOM IT MAY CONCERN:

I, Sam Jones, being of sound mind and body due hereby state that never at any time did I combine, conspire, or agree to possess cocaine with the intent to distribute with Raymond Hicks. In my opinion Raymond Hicks is one of the most respected individuals within the community. For many years he has demonstrated great concern for our neigborhood's youth and elderly. For the past two years my mother has help organized and chaperon the feast on Memorial Day that Mr. Hicks has held for kids that less fortunate than the others at Franklin Park. I cannot imagine that Mr. Hicks would ever, or has ever been involve in any illegal activity. I pray this statement will assist in freeing Raymond Hicks, who is innocent man.

Sincerely,

Sam Jones

The foregoing instrument was acknowledged before me this 14th day of MARCH 2001, by Sam Jones who had produced Federal Detention Center - Miami, Florida Inmate card #: 55345-004 as identification and who is not personally known by me.

DEFENDANT'S
EXHIBIT

5

OFFICIAL NOTARY SEAL
ELIZABETH M GARCIA
NOTARY PUBLIC STATE OF FLORIDA
COMMISSION NO. CC761230
MY COMMISSION EXP. JULY 20,2002

Notary Public - State of Florida

Elizabeth M. Garcia
Notary Public - State of Florida

Document #22, cont.

# Raymond Hicks

I, Asia Nelson, being of sound mind and body due hereby state that never at any time did I combine, conspire, confederate, or agree to possess cocaine with intent to distribute with Raymond Hicks. In my opinion Ramond Hicks is one of the most respected individuals within the community. I was incarcerated at the Broward jail during the period when Mr. Hicks was Correctional Officer. Mr. Hicks encouraged me to return to my family, and become productive member of society. His words touched my heart and brought tears to my eyes. I firmly beleive Mr. Hicks would never, nor has been ever been involve in illegal activity. I personally witness Mr. Hicks helped the neighborhood's youth and elderly. Mr. Hicks is not the alleged person that the government has made him to be. I pray this statement will assist in freeing Raymond Hicks an innocent man, who does not deserve this type of harsh treatment.

Sincerely,

*Asia Nelson*
Asia Nelson

The foregoing instrument was acknowledged before me this 27th day of March 2001, by Asa Nelson who had produced Federal Detention Center – Miami, Florida Inmate card #: 55401-004 as identification and who is not personally known by me.

*Elizabeth M Garcia*
Notary Public – State of Florida

OFFICIAL NOTARY SEAL
ELIZABETH M GARCIA
NOTARY PUBLIC STATE OF FLORIDA
COMMISSION NO. CC761230
MY COMMISSION EXP. JULY 20,2002

*Elizabeth M Garcia*
Notary Public – State of Florida

Document #22, cont.

App-36

# I'M STILL STANDING

<u>TO WHOM IT MAY CONCERN:</u>

I, Elliot Aiken, being of sound mind and body due hereby state that never at any time did I combine, conspire, or agree to possess cocaine with intent to distribute with Raymond Hicks. In my opinion I feel that the Broward Sheriff's Office has a lot to do with his incarceration. I remember hearing at the gym about a lawsuit he had pending against B.S.O. Ramond Hicks is one of our most respected individuals in the community. Mr. Hicks would never as stated in the government's discovery, use his position to "badge himself out of trouble" or be involved in any illegal activity. I pray this statement will assist in freeing Raymond Hicks who is a one hundred percent innocent man.

Sincerely,

Elliot Aiken

The foregoing instrument was acknowledged before me this 27th day of March 2001, by Elliot Aiken who had produced Federal Detention Center - Miami, Florida Inmate card #: 13058-018 as identification and who is not personally known by me.

Notary Public - State of Florida

Elizabeth M. Garcia
Notary Public - State of Florida

**DEFENDANT'S EXHIBIT**
2

Document #22, cont.

App-37

# Raymond Hicks

**U.S. Department of Justic**
**Federal Bureau of Prisor**

*Federal Detention C.*
*33 N.E. 4th S*
*Miami, Fl 33132*

Jan. 18 , 2001

Re:   Raymond Hicks
      Reg. No.55347-004

To Whom it May Concern:

Mr. R. Hicks   is currently incarcerated in the Federal Bureau of Prisons, at the Federal Detention Center in Miami, Florida. Mr.R. Hicks has worked as an orderly and has proven to be responsible and willing to perform any duties as requested. Moreover, Mr.Hicks   has always volunteered to help staff whenever he has seen or has been informed that assistance is needed. He has always conducted himself in a respectable manner towan staff and his fellow inmates. Finally, Mr. Hicks   has not received any disciplinary reports and in my opinion, he is a hard working and well rounded individual.

Correctional Counselor
S. McCann

Document #23 (see Ch. 8, p. 68)

App-38

**UNITED STATES GOVERNMEN**

# memorandum

FEDERAL DETENTION CEN
33 N. E. 4th. 5
MIAMI, FL 3.

DATE: 7/3/01

REPLY TO
ATTN OF: R. Akins, Senior Officer

SUBJECT: Inmate Assistance during Medical Emergency

TO: M. Wetzel, Warden

Thru: R. Yanes, Lieutenant

On 6/20/01, on Unit C -West, at approximately 7:00 pm inmate Harley, Donald #35635-118 went into seizure on the recreation yard. Inmate Lurry, Kenneth #51861-004 notified me of the emergency. I proceeded to the recreation yard and notified Control Center of the emergency. When I approached the scene inmate Hicks, Raymond #55347-004 had rolled inmate Harley onto his side, to prevent him from swallowing his tongue. As I cleared the unit, inmate Hicks continued to hold inmate Harley's hand and assure him help was on the way. Medical staff and the Operations Lieutenant arrived on the unit and escorted inmate Harley to medical for 911 evacuation. The quick thinking of inmate Hicks definitely made a difference in the saving of inmate Harley's life.

Document #23, cont.

App-39

# Raymond Hicks

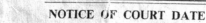

## NOTICE OF COURT DATE
### IN THE CIRCUIT/COUNTY COURT
### IN AND FOR BROWARD COUNTY, FLORIDA

STATE OF FLORIDA

vs

HICKS, RAYMOND

YOU ARE HEREBY NOTIFIED THAT THE FOLLOWING CASE(S) HAS BEEN SET FOR HEARING:

CASE NUMBER: 04000243MM20A          NOTICE TO APPEAR NO.:

TRAFFIC CITATION NUMBER:

TYPE:   NON-JURY TRIAL

JUDGE:   STEVEN P DELUCA                    *PROPER ATTIRE REQUIRED

LOCATION:   NORTH SATELLITE COURTHOUSE
            1600 WEST HILLSBORO BLVD
            DEERFIELD BEACH          FL  33442

DATE:   03/25/2004  TIME:   9:00 A.M.  COURTROOM:   0002

PLEASE BE GOVERNED ACCORDINGLY

HOWARD C. FORMAN
CLERK OF THE CIRCUIT/COUNTY COURT

DATE NOTICED:   03/08/2004

DEFENDANT'S APPEARANCE IS REQUIRED AND MANDATORY.
THE FAILURE OF THE DEFENDANT TO APPEAR ON THE DATE AND TIME
NOTED HEREIN SHALL RESULT IN THE ESTREATURE OF ANY BOND.
NOTE: IF THERE ARE ANY QUESTIONS CALL   (954) 712-7899

***The hiring of an attorney is an important decision.  Should you
need help in finding an attorney, you can call the Broward County
Bar Association for an attorney referral at (954) 764-8040.
*******************************************************************

PARTIES NOTIFIED:
DEFENDANT:   HICKS, RAYMOND
+ ATTORNEY:   VINIKOOR, DAVID G     OAKLAND PARK     3131 NW 43 PLACE
                                                     FL 33309
                                    FT LAUDERDALE    420 SE 12TH ST
                                                     FL 33316-1902

935  2

Document #23, cont.

AO 245A (Rev. 7/87) Judgment of Acquittal

## UNITED STATES DISTRICT COURT

SOUTHERN _____ DISTRICT OF _____ FLORIDA

CLARENCE MADDOX
CLERK U.S. DIST. CT.
S.D. OF FLA. FT. LAUDD.

UNITED STATES OF AMERICA

v.

RAYMOND HICKS

**JUDGMENT OF ACQUITTAL**

CASE NUMBER: 00-6162-CR-ROETTGER

The Defendant was found not guilty. IT IS ORDERED that the Defendant is acquitted, discharged, and any bond exonerated.

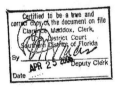

Signature of Judicial Officer

NORMAN C. ROETTGER
Name and Title of Judicial Officer

26 Sep 2001
Date

Certified to be a true and
correct copy of the document on file
Clarence Maddox, Clerk,
U.S. District Court
Southern District of Florida
By _____ Deputy Clerk
Date APR 25 2006

Document #23, cont.

# Raymond Hicks

# J.A.M. Youth Connection, Inc.

*"Our Youth are Destroyed Due to Lack of Knowledge"*

March 12, 2004

To Whom It May Concern:

It has always been my belief that certain people cross our paths for a reason. While it is unclear to me what the future holds, I am confident 1st Sergeant Raymond Hicks is someone I will forever hold in high regard, and be among those I call friend.

As I observed him on March 11, 2004, receiving the prestigious J.M. Family, African American Achievers Award, I was filled with pride because he was a member of the Elite Leadership Military Academy team. The cadets in attendance ran to embrace him after the program because of their love and respect for this very special man.

At first glance, 1st Sergeant Hicks can be intimidating with his voice and size, but it is the heart of Hicks that leaves the most lasting impression. He is a natural at motivating our cadets to be their best by encouraging them, sharing personal stories, and telling him daily that he loves them.

Drill Sergeant Hicks has had his share of troubles. His story is an inspiration, and one he imparts with great humility and thankfulness to God. He is a man of integrity and faith. If you are looking for an honest, highly skilled professional, you need to look no further.

On a more personal note, as an administrator, you must sometimes make unpopular decisions. I always felt, even in the tough times, that Drill Sergeant "had my back' and supported and respected me.

He is a family man, devoted to his wife, daughters and son. His caring and selfless attitude transcends to the workplace, as he has became the father figure to many of our cadets.

Without hesitation or reservation, I would recommend 1st Sergeant Raymond Hicks for any position for which he is qualified. Truly, he would be an asset to any organization.

Sincerely,

Lynda J. Browne
School Administrator

**Elite Leadership Military Academy • JBC Scared Straight Program**
**3403 NW 9th Avenue • Ft. Lauderdale, FL • 33309**
**Office (954) 766-9900 • Fax (954) 735-3888**

# Document #23, cont.

Made in the USA
Charleston, SC
28 December 2015